# INFORMATION SYSTEMS AND NETWORKS

# INFORMATION SYSTEMS AND NETWORKS

## Design and Planning Guidelines of Informatics for Managers, Decision Makers and Systems Analysts

### K. SAMUELSON

*Information Processing-Informatics, Stockholm University and Royal Institute of Technology, Stockholm*

### H. BORKO

*Graduate School of Library and Information Science, University of California, Los Angeles*

### G. X. AMEY

*Information Processing Systems, Defence Scientific Information Service, Ottawa*

1977

NORTH-HOLLAND PUBLISHING COMPANY
AMSTERDAM · NEW YORK · OXFORD

Library of Congress Catalog Card Number: 75-40169
North-Holland ISBN: 0 7204 0407 X


*Published by:*
North-Holland Publishing Company – Amsterdam, New York, Oxford


*Sole distributors for the U.S.A. and Canada:*
Elsevier/North-Holland Inc.
52 Vanderbilt Avenue
New York, NY 10017


**Library of Congress Cataloging in Publication Data**

Samuelson, Kjell.
  Information systems and networks.

  Bibliography: p.
  Includes index.
  1. Information storage and retrieval systems.
2. Management information systems. 3. Information net-
works. I. Borko, Harold, joint author. II. Amey,
G. X., 1929–    joint author. III. Title.
Z699.S322    658.4'03    75-40169
ISBN 0 7204 0407 X


Printed in The Netherlands

# *Foreword*

The following book text was written under a UNESCO-sponsored contract given to FID/TM, the committee for Theory and Methods of Systems, Cybernetics and Information Networks. The work has been carried out by three FID/TM members from Canada, Sweden and USA respectively, and each author contributes about one third of the edited book. The sections on purpose, analysis, planning are mainly Professor Borko's material, while practice, operations, coordination were originated by Dr. Amey and networks, structuring, development, perspectives by Dr. Samuelson, who also did the editing.

As the book title indicates our purpose has been to present practical guidelines of informatics for the planning, design and management of general systems for processing, storage, retrieval and dissemination of information and knowledge. Other purposes of this book on Information Systems and Networks are to serve as an advisory tool and for education and training in developing countries. Moreover, when it comes to the very new field of information networks, almost all nations in the world can be regarded as developing. The topics actually have such a wide scope that each of the chapter sections and subsections could be subject to consultant work resulting in a book as thick as this one. In order not to make the presentation "bulky" the authors have avoided writing about some existing operational document handling systems since they have been described elsewhere. Few, if any, of these represent ultimate designs and their performance and life-cycles should change with experience before an appropriate analysis could be printed. However, as authors we give bibliographic references to case studies of such information systems. The book text also indicates that a major part of the work toward implementing international Information Systems and Networks is a matter of creating methodology and design principles just as much as financing the technology that in fact already has arrived.

*Dr. Kjell Samuelson*

Chairman of FID/TM
(TM: Theory and Methods of Systems,
Cybernetics and Information Networks)

# Contents

CHAPTER 1

# *Introduction*

Information is a great national and international resource, but like the raw material that it is, information must first be processed and distributed before it can be put to productive use. Scientific and technological knowledge has been expanding rapidly during the past two decades, and there is every likelihood that the growth rate will continue to increase. This knowledge is very costly to produce. It has been estimated that in the United States alone, the annual expenditure for research and development exceeds $27 billion (SATCOM, 1969). Clearly, this is a valuable and expensive resource that cannot be allowed to go unused. The knowledge gained from research provides the basis for new scientific and technological advances. The effectiveness of future work in universities, and in governmental and industrial laboratories rests on the availability of past knowledge, and this in turn is dependent upon the network of information transfer resources in the community.

In the simpler societies of the past, knowledge accumulated more slowly, and the scholar was able to assimilate new information at a reasonably leisurely pace. Unfortunately, this is no longer true. The proliferation of useful research coupled with the number of people involved in science and technology have overburdened the traditional information

1

services to a point where they can no longer assume the entire burden of information handling in today's society. These traditional services must be supplemented with other institutional forms that are designed to meet the new and expanded needs of today's society.

These new concepts for improved information transfer are in their early stages of development. Much experimentation needs to be done, but some progress has been made, and some direction can be provided. The problem is severe; large volumes of information are being produced; existing information transfer channels are being overloaded; as a result, information tends to be lost or ignored and unused. We cannot wait for the perfect solution; some steps need to be taken now to unclog the channels and improve the flow of information. The desired outcome is more responsive information systems that would be able to acquire, process, store, and disseminate information to all who need it at the time they need it. Perhaps this goal will never be fully achieved, but one must try, and with effort, progress will be made.

It is the purpose of this text to provide guidelines that would aid the manager-decision maker, the systems analyst and others in the planning and designing of an effective information system.

## 1.1. Definitions

Since this field of study is still an evolving one, no definitive, authoritative definitions exist on which all practitioners would agree. Nevertheless, in order to provide a common basis for the discussion that follows, working definitions of a few basic terms are provided. It is particularly important to understand the relationship between information science, systems analysis and design, and information systems as these terms are used in this book and its glossary.

*Information Science* is an interdisciplinary science that investigates the properties and behavior of information, the forces governing the flow of information, and the means of processing it for optimum accessibility and usability. As an interdisciplinary science it draws upon the skills and knowledge of behavioral scientists, cyberneticians, general system theorists, librarians, computer architects, engineers, etc.

*System* is an organized collection of men, machines, and material required to accomplish a specific purpose and tied together by communication links (that often constitute a network).

*Information System* is that combination of human and computer-based capital resources which results in the collection, storage, retrieval, communication and use of data for the purpose of efficient management (planning, decision-making, reporting and control) of operations in organizations.

*Information Technology* involves the application of tools and techniques of information science to the operation problems of an information system. Computers, telecommunications and micromedia are typical examples.

*Systems Analysis* is a formal procedure for examining a complex process or organization by reducing it to its human and material resources and relating these component parts to each other and to the unit as a whole in accordance with agreed-upon performance criteria. It is both a general approach to problem-solving and a group of scientific techniques drawn from many fields and disciplines that are used in solving particular problems.

*Systems Design* is a formal procedure for combining human resources, equipment, techniques, information, data and work procedures into an integrated construct (sometimes a network) in order to facilitate organizational performance. *Informatics* and *Networks*, defined on pp. 71, 103, 134, 139.

## 1.2. The systems approach

An information system is a very complex structure composed of many interrelating units and functions. The most effective technique which can be used for studying such an organization is systems analysis. This is not a new technique, and although the term has a modern ring, the underlying ideas can be traced back into ancient history.

The Babylonians, Greeks and Phoenicians, among others, viewed the universe as a system of interacting phenomena. They went as far as attempting to apply their rudimentary mathematics to the understanding and prediction of the relationship between the celestial phenomena and the everyday events in the world about them.

In more recent times, the physical, biological and social sciences have approached the problems within their respective purviews in terms of system concepts and constructs. Thus, for example, both the atom and the universe are dealt with as systems; both the individual man and the whole of society are dealt with scientifically as biological, psychological, and sociocultural systems. One of the major problems today is to discover the principles of interaction among such systems. The exploration of generalized features and similarities between living systems (Miller, 1971, 1976) or other diversified subsystems is a branch of science itself referred to as "General Systems Research" and represented throughout the years in volumes of the *General Systems Yearbook* (1958–75) and many journal articles.

Traditionally, scientific research has been conducted in the university environment. Such efforts have been oriented primarily toward the search for, and the accumulation of, basic knowledge and not necessarily toward the solution of specific problems. A change occurred during World War II, at which time highly qualified scientific and engineering talent from all countries were called away from the classroom, and from the traditional laboratory, in order to apply science and technology to further the war and defence effort. This unprecedented concentration of talent developed such military systems as radar, ballistic missiles, and atomic energy as well as improvements in antibiotics, medicine and surgery. One of the lesser publicized results of this wartime scientific and engineering effort was the emergence of the powerful new disciplines of systems analysis and operations research.

The systems approach is a very broad concept, and it can be applied to a wide variety of problems. Typically, systems analysis is used in government and industry as a procedure for finding the best method—or at least one of the better alternative methods—for achieving a reasonable solution. When used in corporate planning, systems analysis is a contributing part of the firm's policy decision-making procedures. In information science, systems analysis is used both as a general approach to the study of information systems and as an application of scientific techniques to the solution of specific information transfer problems.

System studies consist of the following essential activities:

(1) Planning and project definition,
(2) Analysis of existing and related systems,
(3) Design of appropriate alternative systems,
(4) Design evaluation,
(5) Pilot system implementation and evaluation,
(6) Operational system implementation and evaluation.

The next four chapters of this book will be concerned primarily with the planning and analysis phases, and for these phases a more detailed discussion of the activities involved will be presented.

# CHAPTER 2

# General Characteristics of Systems Analysis

The systems approach is multi-disciplinary, problem solving oriented, and it utilizes quantitative management science techniques to develop and evaluate a spectrum of solutions for complex, usually long-range, problems (Adelson, 1968).

Further statements about the systems approach are expressed by Churchman (1968) who declares:

(i) What is in the nature of systems is a continuing perception and deception, a continuing re-viewing of the world, of the whole system, and of its components.

(ii) The systems approach begins when first you see the world through the eyes of another.

(iii) The systems approach goes on to discovering that every world view is terribly restricted.

No doubt, the above statements are valid and hold true for documentation services and libraries or in fact, modern information systems and networks as well. These general conditions call for a system study.

## 2.1. Multi-disciplinary orientation

The methodology employed in system studies is multi-disciplinary in nature. Usually a team of skilled professional people, both generalists and specialists, is required to examine the problem domain and, in a specified period of time, achieve a thorough understanding of the system so as to evaluate not only how it functions but also *how* it might be made to function. The team members will have different skills and training, but in addition they must have enough of a common background so that they can communicate effectively about their common task. Team work, as well as individual excellence, is essential. The essence of the team is its task orientation and purposiveness. The methodology should be understood by each of the members, and all should operate on the basis of reasonable but demanding mutual expectations.

## 2.2. Problem solving orientation

The systems approach is a problem oriented one. It is a highly creative process, and the outcome is dependent upon the people involved as well as on the resources available. The solutions arrived at are not likely to be uniquely implicit in the data or derivable from the stated objectives; however, they must be generated so as to be consistent with the data and objectives. Moreover, in any given situation, the available data and theoretical framework are likely to be incomplete and somewhat ambiguous so that certainty is out of the question. Imagination, judgement and courage are needed. The set of possible future environments in which proposed solutions must remain valid have to be imagined, and their potential effects evaluated. Alternative solutions must be generated, characterized and evaluated. Even the way the problem domain under study is subdivided for conceptual manageability is a matter of considerable importance that demands responsible judgement and originality. The traditional subdivisions along jurisdictional or organizational lines, or in terms of standard academic disciplines, are not necessarily the best and are certainly not the only options. Each aspect has its place and must be considered. Clearly, creativity is called for at many points in the process of achieving a problem solution.

Numerous writers and users of the systems approach have recognized the explicit relationship between systems analysis and scientific problem solving. Polya in his book *How To Solve It* (Polya, 1957) provides a succinct outline of problem solving methodology. It consists, he says, of the following four steps:

(1) Understanding the problem—
Identify the unknown, the data and the conditions in the problem.
(2) Divising a plan—
Find the connection between the data and the unknown; consider related problems and intermediate connections.
(3) Carrying out the plan—
Implement the plan for achieving the solution and checking each step in the process.
(4) Looking back—
Examine and evaluate the solution obtained.

Polya was not concerned with systems analysis, but the procedures he outlined are those that all systems analysts follow. Some of the most frequently cited works in this field are those of Stanford Optner, a systems analyst. He defines a system as a "device for examining the process of problem-solving" (Optner, 1965, p. 3). He, too, lists a number of steps to be followed which are particularily helpful in understanding the problem and devising a plan of action. These steps include (Optner, 1965, p. 21):

(1) The problem process must be flow-charted, showing the principal decision points.

(2) Details of the principal decision process steps must be described.

(3) Detailed presentation of data, data relationships, and the procedural steps by which data were evaluated must be part of any solution.

(4) The principal alternatives and how they were generated must be demonstrable, and the criteria for their evaluation must be fully stated.

Properly practised, the systems approach provides a means for tapping the creativity and judgement of a broad assortment of relevant professional and technical disciplines. One of its major advantages is that it provides a framework into which the inputs from these diverse sources may flow usefully, and thus the procedure insures that the problem domain will be examined from many different aspects and in the broadest possible context.

## 2.3. Quantitative management science orientation

Systems analysis is a tool of management to be used as an aid for organizational planning and decision making. Obviously the tool, i.e. systems analysis, does not make the decision; management makes the decision using all available information. The systems approach provides a method for integrating an empirical data gathering approach with a theoretical framework in order to solve practical problems. Empiricism, theory and pragmatics are combined into the systems approach.

### 2.3.1. Empiricism

Great reliance is placed on data; not just the data on the

subject itself but also data about the relevant practices, functions, interactions, and impinging characteristics of related organizations. Generally large masses of statistics will have to be collected. Where appropriate, computers are used to process, store and analyze these figures. However, a great deal of the information that can be collected is not readily quantifiable; qualitative data are extremely important, and so techniques have been devised for their effective utilization. These analytical methods include data distribution models and various methods of analyses such as cost/performance/benefit studies. Not only do the models aid in understanding the already collected data, but they may give direction to the search for new data.

### 2.3.2. Theory

Without theory, data cannot be fully exploited. If theory does not exist, other less precise formulations will have to be used to represent the relationships among relevant factors. One of the functions of the systems approach is to gather, and to the extent possible, organize the relevant theoretical work from various academic disciplines that relate directly or indirectly to the subject. Where well developed theories or models are lacking, the organization responsible for the work should note the kinds of models that are needed and proceed either to develop them or to encourage their development by other individuals or organizations. Only in this way will the effectiveness of the systems approach improve.

### 2.3.3. Pragmatics

A crucial characteristic of the systems approach is that it is action-oriented. Its products are intended to be useful in the world of practical affairs. Data are gathered to do more than inform; models are used to do more than elucidate a relationship, and ideas must be more than just clever or insightful. All activities must be goal-oriented, and are engaged in because they are instrumental in fulfilling a set of purposes or in responding to a set of real needs. Purposes and needs are those of the agencies or organizations for whom the work is being done. The task of these organizations is to make appropriate decisions about the allocation of resources, the development of programs, and the formulation of policies. These decisions have an impact on the interests of many other kinds of organizations and individuals, and those organizations and individuals in turn have economic, professional, social, political and personal stakes in the outcome. Thus, an adequate understanding of the character of each organization must be generated by the system team. If the systems approach is to be fully utilized, the organizations involved will need to participate actively in the process of study, analysis and development.

## 2.4. Value and limitations

Although the process of systems analysis is straightforward in concept, it can be exceedingly complex and difficult in application. It must be emphasized that systems analysis is not a panacea. It is not a black box into which one drops problems at one end and automatically receives solutions at the other. It is, as was pointed out, a framework in which a multi-disciplinary group of scientists, engineers and technicians can achieve a unified problem-oriented focus, and this common research orientation maximizes the possibilities for achieving successful solutions of complex problems. The real value of systems analysis lies in the fact that it forces a manager to structure his thinking to the problem at hand, to prepare a solution given a particular set of circumstances, to prepare alternatives and to establish requirements.

The promise of the systems approach is substantial but not unlimited. In systems analysis the real world is presented as a model, and a model is one level removed from reality. Although every effort is made to simulate the basic parameters, the model can never include all aspects of the real world. Thus an optimum solution to the problem, as defined in the model, may not work in the real world. On the other hand, it is only by means of models that one can understand the world in all of its complexities.

Systems analysis cannot solve all problems; it cannot and/or will not:

(a) provide a set of precise rules and procedures for arriving at incontestably correct solutions;

(b) provide correct solutions by a sophisticated analysis of inaccurate or unreliable data;

(c) provide a system of values that would imply the proper objectives or goals that ought to be achieved;

(d) replace judgement; system studies can at best provide a basis for making better informed judgements, but the methodology should not be used as a replacement for judgement;

(e) replace the managerial decision process; systems analysts sometimes make decisions, but foremost they provide information which can be used by management for making decisions;

(f) produce maximally useful results, or solutions, to operational problems, without the active and continuing participation of management personnel from the client organization.

In summary, systems analysis is a methodological tool that can be used very effectively in solving complex problems, but it is only a tool, and one should not expect a tool—even a versatile tool—to be equally effective in all situations. More importantly, one should not confuse the tool with the solution or the method with the results.

# CHAPTER 3

# Phase I: Planning

In undertaking a systems study, the first and most crucial step is planning, for without adequate preparation the study is bound to fail. Planning begins with management's recognition that a change in existing practice is needed. The focus of the change may be a desire to provide new services, or to undertake new projects so as to improve and expand existing services, or to cut costs and provide the same service more efficiently, etc. A desire for a change does not make it so. If existing procedures are to be modified, then someone must be assigned the task to study the existing system, to propose modifications, to determine the potential costs and benefits of these modifications, and to report the findings. This is also called the *feasibility study*.

Usually some senior person from the management staff is assigned the responsibility to initiate and supervise the study. He is given a budget and a time when the study is to be completed. In order to carry out the project, he will have to obtain the services of a qualified technical staff. The size and composition of this technical staff will vary depending upon the complexity of the project. Generally the staff will include one or more systems analysts. Thus even before a systems study can be undertaken, a number of prior activities must take place at the top management level. These are:

(1) the recognition that a change in the existing mode of operations is desirable;

(2) the appointment of a project manager responsible for carrying out the feasibility study;

(3) the allocation of funds for the initiation of the study and the setting of a completion date;

(4) the appointment of a technical staff.

Once these preliminary steps have been taken and a systems analysis and design team established, planning can begin. Planning is a joint responsibility of the management staff and the technical staff working together as a team. Some of the planning functions are primarily management, some are mainly technical tasks, and some must be joint responsibilities (see Fig. 1).

## 3.1. Management responsibilities

A representative of management must be an active and contributing member of the systems study team. His role is to contribute a management orientation to the study effort. It is his responsibility to specify the objectives and system goals, and he must identify the constraints and restrictions within which these goals are to be achieved. In addition this person (or persons) acts as a liaison representative between the members of the systems project and the rest of the organization. If the goals are not useful, if the constraints are unrealistic, and if there is inadequate communication between the study team and the organization, then the entire systems analysis and design effort will fail to achieve useful results regardless of its technical qualities.

### 3.1.1. Determination of objectives and system goals

Management's initial responsibility is to specify the ob-

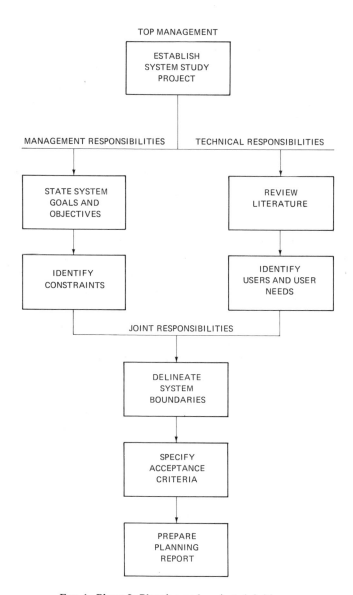

FIG. 1. Phase I: Planning and project definition.

jectives to be achieved, the operational problems to be solved, and the new services to be provided. This statement of basic aims will guide the entire study effort. Once the objectives have been defined, the process of systems analysis focuses on translating this statement of needs into a detailed set of operational goals. During this stage the organization's goals are converted into specific measurable situations which, when achieved, will satisfy the defined needs in operational terms.

### 3.1.2. Identification of constraints

No system operates with unlimited resources, and so during this initial planning stage, management must also specify the constraints, or the limiting conditions, which must be observed in achieving the desired objectives.

Three sets of constraints can be identified. The first deals with limiting conditions which are outside the organization and thus beyond the control of its management. These may be designated as *environmental constraints*. The second set is *organizational constraints* which are under internal control. These include the funds available for the purchase of new equipment, operating costs, personnel training programs, etc. The third set is *operational constraints* and consists of standards that the system must meet in order to be acceptable, e.g. the number of units to be processed each day.

Constraints set limits to the scope of the systems study and tie it to reality considerations.

## 3.2. Technical staff responsibilities

During the initial planning phase, the technical staff has two major responsibilities: (1) to review relevant design literature, and (2) to become acquainted with the people who will be using the information system, with their needs for information, and with their methods of search and inquiry.

### 3.2.1. Review of the literature

The reasons for reviewing the literature should be obvious. Essentially, a literature review enables one to benefit from the experience of others, to utilize the work that others have done, and to avoid the mistakes that others have made. No new project should be undertaken without first making a thorough search of the relevant literature, and this should be especially true in the field of information science.

### 3.2.2. Identification of the system users and their needs

Every information system is designed to meet the requirements of its users. An essential part of the planning function consists of specifying the various categories of people for whom the system is designed and who will be using it. The user groups must be identified, defined and delimited. For example, if one were dealing with an information system consisting of chemical literature, the probable users may be research chemists, bench chemists, pharmacologists, drug control or project managers, etc. Not only must the system provide services to these different types of users, but they will use the system to obtain different categories of information. These too must be identified.

The technical staff is responsible for providing the design team with factual data on:

(1) How information needs are currently being met.
(2) The inadequacies of these proceedings.
(3) The added services that would be desired.

Generally, user needs are studied by means of surveys and questionaires. This is a complex task and one which should be undertaken early in the planning process.

### 3.3. Joint responsibilities

Even though both the management and the technical staffs have been assigned primary responsibility for certain tasks, the planning function is really a joint responsibility of the entire system study group. A great deal of interaction, at all levels, is essential, for the system goals and procedures are dynamic concepts needing constant attention and modification.

Specific areas of joint responsibility, for both the management and the technical staffs, lie in (1) the delineation of the system boundaries, (2) the specification of acceptance criteria, and (3) the preparation of the Phase I: Project Planning Report.

### 3.3.1. Delineation of system boundaries

A system, it has been pointed out, consists of men, material and machines organized to accomplish a specific purpose. But no system is complete in itself; every system is part of a still larger system. Thus a local library can be part of a regional library system which is part of a national system, etc. A most important planning task is to delimit and place boundaries about the system to be studied. If the system is made too large, too inclusive, the study effort will become unwieldy and overly expensive. If the system is defined too narrowly, significant factors will be excluded, and the desired efficiencies will not be achieved.

The systems analysis effort must explicitly separate the system to be studied from the embedding environment which is defined as everything outside the system. There are seldom rules for optimizing the boundaries of a system. This is more of an art than a science, and since both management and technical problems are involved in the decision, the responsibility for setting the boundaries should be shared jointly. For example, should the designers of an information system be concerned with the selection and screening of material, or should the system study begin with the processing of documents that have already been acquired? Where does the system begin? The boundaries which separate the system from the environment must be agreed upon.

There is a related task that needs to be done, and that is the identification of the component subsystems and their relationships to each other and to the system as a whole. Although the major information handling subsystems, e.g. selection, acquistition, cataloging, etc., are generally easy to identify, in practice it is often difficult to determine their interface relationships. Nevertheless, a successful systems analysis effort requires that these subsystems be delineated so that they could be studied, i.e. analyzed, as units and their interrelationships specified. Again, since these subsystems generally function as management units, the setting of the subsystem boundaries should be a joint team effort.

## 3.3.2. Specification of system acceptance criteria

During the Planning Phase of the study, the systems analyst must work together with the management staff to specify the criteria by which the performance of the system will be evaluated. It is not adequate to state that the system should be "useful, efficient and inexpensive to operate". These are not criteria, for there is no way of measuring performance against such general statements. Performance criteria must be stated in operational terms, using minimum and maximum limiting values within which the system must operate if it is to be acceptable, e.g. between 100 and 150 documents must be processed each day; 90% of user requests must be fulfilled in less than 15 minutes, etc.

The agreed-upon performance criteria will be used both in measuring the effectiveness of the existing system and evaluating the advantages of the new design. It is important that these acceptance criteria be specified in the planning phase of the system study effort rather than in the subsequent analysis and design phases. The criteria should be independent of actual operating characteristics.

### 3.3.3. Preparation of the Phase I report: Planning and project definition

The planning phase concludes with the preparation of a report in which the various aspects of the planning process are clearly stated. These aspects include system goals, objectives and constraints. Also included is a review of the literature, the lessons learned from this review and the implications relevant to the design of the proposed new system. The preparation of this report is a joint effort to which all members of the system study group contribute. It is a formal document which must be submitted for approval to the top management of the sponsoring organization. The report provides management with an opportunity to review the work of the system study team, and if this work is satisfactory, to authorize the beginning of the next phase of the study—the detailed analysis of the existing system—if one exists.

# CHAPTER 4

# Phase II: Analysis of Existing Procedures

Once the planning task has been completed and the Phase I report accepted by top management, the system study effort concentrates on a detailed examination of the existing system. It may be argued that since a new system is being planned, that there is no existing system, or if there is one, it is known to be inadequate, and that therefore it would be a waste of effort to examine the present procedures. This is a fallacious argument. Only rarely does one have an opportunity to design a new system from the very beginning and even in this case, the new design is rarely a radical departure from some rudimentary practices that are in operation. For example, if the problem were to design an international cancer research information system, it can be assumed that no such system exists. However, this does not mean that cancer researchers do not have access to medical information in their field. Their existing methods of publishing, disseminating and retrieving information should be studied. Only when one thoroughly understands current practices can one suggest improvements.

The analysis is conducted by the system study group. This is a technical task, and the systems analysts are assigned the responsibility for conducting the study. The management personnel on the team generally guide and monitor the work and serve as resource persons to answer questions and explain the organization's policy.

## 4.1. Requirements

As has been stated in the preceding paragraph, the prime purpose for conducting an analysis of the existing procedures is to gain an understanding of the current methods of operation and of the organization's policies that have a bearing on the system. The analysis is essentially a fact gathering and descriptive procedure. The analyst must:

(a) describe the organizational units in which the work is performed;

(b) specify the input, processing and output procedures;

(c) specify and describe any exceptions to the routine procedures;

(d) assemble the forms used in performing and monitoring the various activities;

(e) obtain pertinent statistical data on the number and variety of units processed by the system per unit of time;

(f) obtain pertinent cost figures for calculating cost/performance/benefit ratios;

(g) survey the users of the system to determine the benefits derived;

(h) identify processing bottlenecks and other problem areas.

The preceding list is indicative of the kinds of descriptive data that should be obtained during the course of the analysis phase of the system study effort. It is not meant to be an inclusive or a complete listing; it does, however, provide specific illustrations of what is meant by "an understanding of current methods of operation" as implemented in a system study.

## 4.2. Methods

The systems approach is interdisciplinary, and the methods employed in conducting a systems study are many and varied. This survey does not attempt to explain or describe the methodology. Like the previous section, it simply lists the techniques, arranged by topic areas, together with some brief annotations.

The essential task is to gather all the necessary data that will enable the systems analyst to understand and describe:

(a) the organization of the system,
(b) the methods of operation,
(c) the quality and quantity of the work being done,
(d) the costs involved;
(e) the benefits of the services as perceived by the users.

Data on all these topics must be gathered, recorded and analysed. To accomplish these tasks, the systems analyst relies heavily on the use of various types of displays and charts both for description and analysis.

### 4.2.1. Data gathering and recording techniques

The most common technique used in gathering data is the interview—the systems analyst interviews the people who can provide him with the information he needs. The technique sounds simple, and indeed it is, but there are many pitfalls. The object is not just to gather information; it is to gather accurate and complete information, and to do so in as simple and efficient a manner as is possible while maintaining the good will and active cooperation of those being interviewed. These constraints make the task more difficult, and they require adequate prior preparation on the part of the interviewer. The management representatives on the study team can be of great help by providing information on who to see, who to call for appointments, etc.

In gathering, recording and analyzing the data, the systems analyst uses charts of various kinds. He is a firm believer in the notion that a single picture is worth a thousand words. The chart is the embodiment of the analysis.

*System description.* During the planning phase, the system to be investigated has been described and the major subsystems have been identified. Based upon this information it is possible to draw a system flow chart.

*System flow chart* is a block diagram in which the major functions or processes are represented, and the relationship of one process to another is displayed by arrows showing both the points of interconnection and the direction of information flow. This chart represents an overall diagrammatic view of the tasks performed by the system (e.g., Fig. 2).

Once the tasks are known, a next step is to describe the organization that performs these functions. This description takes the form of a *system organization chart.* The purpose of an organization chart is to graphically display the administrative units of the organization, e.g. divisions, departments, branches, etc., and the hierarchical arrangement of these units within the organization (e.g., Fig. 3).

*Unit description.* These two system charts enable one to see "the big picture", but the level of information needs to be expanded during the detailed analysis that follows. The forms for recording the information remain essentially the same, but the level of detail increases. Each functional unit, which has previously been defined and delimited by boundaries during the planning phase and shown on the system chart, is now analyzed part by part, function by function. Detailed *operational flow charts* are drawn as well as *unit organization charts.* The unit charts must account for every person in the organization, and the flow charts account for every significant task that is performed. The data on which these charts are based is gathered by interviewing the employees that should

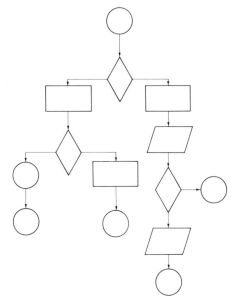

FIG. 2. Flow chart.

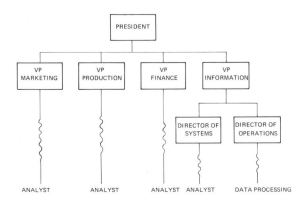

FIG. 3. Organization chart.

be doing the work and the supervisors responsible for having it done.

As an aid in the data gathering task, and as an aid in understanding and describing the tasks that the unit performs, it is helpful to collect all of the forms that either originate in that unit or are processed by that unit. One can prepare a *forms flow chart* which traces the set of forms—all copies— as it moves from one unit to another until it is completely filled out and filed.

The preparation of these unit charts, particularly the operational flow charts, is fairly complex. To insure that all functions performed are accurately presented, the operating and supervising personnel should be allowed to review the descriptions and suggest changes that need to be made.

*Performance measures.* At the same time that the systems analyst is gathering data to describe the organization and functions of the various units, he should also be collecting information on the complexity and quantity of work being done (number of units of each type being processed) and the unit costs. There are a number of ways in which these data can be recorded: Work counts, work log estimates, timing by observation, work sampling, standard performance criteria, etc. Care should be taken to distinguish between peak performance and average performance.

*User benefits.* In the course of a systems analysis, it is not only necessary to determine what is being done, but it is also necessary to determine if the work being done is useful and to measure the extent of the benefits provided to the user. In gathering data on the performance characteristics of the system, interviews were conducted with the employees. To gather data on the benefits, it is necessary to interview the users of the system. Since there are generally many more users than employees, mail questionnaires and surveys are often used in preference to direct interviews. Obviously the questions used must be unambiguous and structured to provide usable data. The construction of questionnaires is itself a specialized subject. It is recommended that expert help be obtained in preparing questionnaires.

*Summary.* To summarize briefly, the description of a system (which is part of the analysis) includes a functional and organizational description of the overall system, a functional and organizational description of each unit, and the collecting of work performance, cost and user benefit measures.

## 4.2.2. *Data analysis techniques*

The primary technique for data gathering is the interview; for data recording, it is the flow chart; and for data analysis it is operations research. Operations research involves the use of mathematically oriented analytical methods for solving operational problems. The objective is to provide management with factual quantitative reports on the relative merits of alternative courses of action. Among the common analytical techniques used in operations research are the following: linear programming, probability theory, information theory, game theory, queuing theory, and the Monte-Carlo method. These are rather specialized complex topics, and they provide the systems analyst with reasonably sophisticated techniques for analyzing the data he has gathered and for evaluating alternative courses of action. The most common criteria used as a basis for evaluation is the cost/performance/benefit analysis.

*Cost/performance* is a measure of cost-efficiency. It measures how much it costs to perform a given task; the lower the cost or the higher the performance, the smaller the ratio and the more efficient the system.

*Cost/benefit* is a measure of cost-effectiveness. It measures the cost of providing a given service (e.g. benefit) to the user; the smaller the cost or the greater the degree of service, the more effective the system.

*Performance/benefit* is another measure of effectiveness. It relates the number of units of work that the system must perform in order to provide the user with the benefits he requires.

Operations research methods as well as cost/performance/benefit measures are important and indeed essential techniques for data analysis. However, it would be erroneous to assume that the systems analyst relies entirely on mathematical methods. Data analysis is after all mainly an intellectual process. It is crucial for the analyst to ask the right questions, for if the wrong questions are asked, no amount of mathematical magic could provide useful answers. The following are some of the essential questions that the analyst should ask as he analyzes the efficiency and the effectiveness of the system (Beach, 1967):

Are the goals and objectives, the purposes of the system, being achieved?
Are things being done the right way?
Are things being done at the right place?
Are things being done in the right amount?
Are things being done in the right order?
Are things being done at the right cost?
Are things being done by the right people, or by the right mix of men and machines?
Are there additional things that should be done?

These are some of the crucial questions to be asked in a systems analysis. Data is gathered to provide answers to these questions. Flow charts describe the work that is being done. Organization charts provide information on who is doing the work. Operations research techniques analyze the data in terms of some of the above questions. Problem areas can now be identified and alternative systems proposed and studied.

### 4.2.3. Preparation of the Phase II report: Analysis of existing procedures

At the conclusion of Phase II, a report is prepared setting forth the results of the analysis. The report enables top management to monitor the results of the analysis, to determine whether or not the study team understands the functions of the organization and has properly identified the problems that need to be solved. If the report is approved, management can then authorize the initiation of the next phase of the study effort which consists of the design and evaluation of alternate systems and procedures for solving the problems and improving operations.

# CHAPTER 5

# Systems Planning and Analysis Procedures in Summary

A useful distinction can be made between systems analysis and systems design; although both are part of the more inclusive activity which may be called a *systems study*. In systems analysis one is primarily concerned with identifying the problems that need to be solved, and with making a detailed study, or analysis, of the organizational units and operations in which these problems reside. This is precisely what is meant by analysis—a complex problem area is divided into smaller units in order to facilitate study and understanding. The systems approach is based upon the scientific method of problem solving. It provides a framework and *methodology* for examining complex problems in a systematic manner and improving the likelihood of achieving a successful solution.

Analysis provides understanding; it does not provide a solution. However, successful solutions are based upon the correct understanding of the problem.

After a proper analysis has been performed, one can consider possible solutions. This is the design phase. During this phase, a number of alternative solutions are generated which could solve the problem and improve operations. The word "alternative" is an important one, for there are many ways of achieving a given objective although not all will be equally efficient. A systems design consists of a description of the reasonable alternatives and a recommendation of the best choice. The criteria for evaluating the alternatives is the set of criteria which has been previously specified during the planning phase of the study. The methods used for design evaluation are procedures similar to those that have been used in the analysis of the existing system. A proposed system is designed, then evaluated.

The systems approach does not stop with the design phase, for if the problem is to be solved, the approved design must be implemented. And again the cycle repeats itself. The new design now becomes the existing system which must be analysed and evaluated. New problems will be identified and new solutions proposed. System studies are continuing, iterative procedures for examining and improving operational systems. The following activities were identified:

(1) Planning,
(2) Analysis,
(3) Design of alternatives,
(4) Design evaluation,
(5) Pilot implementation,
(6) Operational implementation and evaluation.

The topic test and evaluation has become a field of its own. Therefore such details have not been included in the present book. Instead the reader is referred to the current literature included in the bibliography (Samuelson et al., 1974, King and Bryant, 1971).

CHAPTER 6

# Operations and System
# Implementation

People usually feel more secure when working in an essentially static environment. The onset of change is perceived as a threat and tends to call forth a hostile response (Fried, 1972). The management of change calls for considerable skill in dealing with people, a skill which has often been lacking in those called upon to design and implement new information systems. Problems of human behavior related to management information systems designed solely for problem solving often arise because of the system designer's primary concern with system mechanics (Neel, 1971). The literature of the field concerned with computer system development revealed a singular gap with regard to organized thought on preparing the organization of computer systems (McCarn, 1970) until recently. It is now increasingly realized that hardware inadequacies can no longer be blamed for the failure of systems developed in the late sixties (Jacobs, 1972). Where assistance has been sought from use of operations research techniques, acceptance has not been better, due to the acceptance of unrealistic assumptions used in search of an illusory optimum (Wagner, 1971). More appropriately, "satisficing" should be sought instead of "optimizing" (see page 92).

## 6.1. The project manager

Since a management system is a process of people interacting to apply resources to achieve goals (Myers, 1971), the project manager must be, above all things, a competent manager rather than a systems technician. By default, in many cases, the responsibility for overall system development has rested with people whose real expertise lies in the fields of computer systems and software design. The result usually is a system optimized for hardware efficiency at the expense of the human users and operators of the system. Because of his machine-orientation, the software expert and programmer appear to be particularly unsuited for dealing with people and liable to misconceptions concerning the usage and behavioral patterns of the scientists, engineers, and managers, for whom the system is designed.

The management of a dynamic environment has an extensive literature in publications on management and behavioral sciences, but until recently had almost no coverage in the technical journals read by computermen. The appointment of a senior management representative as the nominal project head will not solve the problems inherent in seeking acceptance of innovation, if the person chosen does not have a strong, almost emotional commitment, to the success of the project. In too many cases, the most committed member of the development team is the systems man, whose personal goals and judgment are unlikely to coincide with those of the group for whom the system is being developed. He may not realize, as would an experienced manager, that the members of an organization will feel less threatened by change, if they have some degree of control over their own destiny. It is best for the individual or group to have some self-direction and influence on the impact of change (Fried, 1972). They need to be led rather than pushed into acceptance. As MIT provost J. H. Holloman has said:

There are two ways into which new things come into being .... one is called the push mechanism. You spend a lot of money on a new technology and then try to push it into society and hope, because it is novel or different, that some one will buy the product. It has been very seldom that such a system has worked (Hancon, 1971).

Leadership of high order is asked of the officer with overall responsibility for the success of the project. To provide such leadership is not always a function of the systems man, whose role, as stated earlier in the text, is rather to propose alternative methods the project manager may use in forwarding the project. Ideally, the latter should not water down or delay achievement of objectives through over-emphasis of unanimity amongst participants in the development. He must be able to accept viable disagreements in which more and more people inject their views into decision making (Cleveland, 1972).

## 6.2. System options

In the system analysis phases described earlier, the current system has been examined with a view to determining where application of new technology would be beneficial. This exercise will largely be constrained within the boundary of the subsystem initiating the study (see Section 3.1.2). However, when senior management reviews the results of the systems analyst's feasibility studies with a view to implementation, they are under no such constraint. They may well ask themselves whether large sums of money should be invested in the hopes of incremental improvement of the current system.

There are at least three options generally available:

(1) to develop a totally new system with its own internal organization, its own inputs and outputs;

(2) to produce a version of the existing system, hopefully enhanced by the substitution of elements arising from the application of new technology, for certain of the manual procedures;

(3) to review the prime objectives of the organization as a whole (and not just the operation of the particular subsystem) to determine whether these can better be served by extensions of the current system made possible by application of new technology.

### 6.2.1. Creation of a new system

At first sight, this may not seem possible or desirable. However, a review of the problems involved in trying to adapt old systems to new methods or new objectives, can make this an attractive alternative.

It is worth considering whether the full application of modern technology to any existing system, e.g., a conventional library, may not in fact change the nature of the function so fundamentally as to imply formation of a new entity. The application of computer techniques to accounting operations implies no real change in the library function, which is concerned above all with cataloging, storing and lending of books. The use of computer and micrographic aids however, opens new vistas, concerned not so much with the storage and control of the packages (books, journals, etc.) containing the information, but with the information content itself. The experience arising from attempting to graft the information-function on to existing library structures has been very frustrating (Rees, 1972). There are essential problems of staffing and career opportunities relative to subject specialists vis-a-vis librarians. For example, a system geared to the provision of medical information, of necessity must have at least some medical staff. The status and salary of medical professionals is such that it is difficult to relate them to librarians who are much lower in the hierarchy of an organization. The medical professionals should of course be given the same career opportunities, salary advancements and "chairs" within the information science field as in clinics, hospitals or private practice. Actually, higher management functions are sometimes handled by grant-hustler outsiders holding positions in other fields, and who by empire-building try to manoeuvre the information activities as a diletante's sideline for selfish, power-seeking reasons. It is more important to focus on humanity, motivation and selffulfillment of the personnel actually doing the job rather than the interests of the micropolitical operator. Cases are known where the sound, healthy development and creative progress has been inhibited over 10–15 years by one single minidictatorial empire-builder, whose selfish ignorance has blocked all openings. That is why open systems must be fostered (Beer, 1975). The identical principle goes for any other discipline versus the information science functions (see Section 7.5.1). In order to achieve adequate financing and to ensure participation of competent senior management in system development, it may well be desirable that the information function be transferred to the directive level of the organizational structure (Fig. 3) much higher than is customary for library functions (Waggener, 1974). The very use of a computer sometimes suggests integrating of all information functions within an organization into a single but distributed corporate data base. Many a development project of high intrinsic merit has failed due to stop-and-go financing or general lack of interest of the decision-makers. History confirms how various odd people handled libraries before librarians existed. The task of determining the significance of a new type of information service, relative to the channels of communication of total organizations, may well be beyond the capabilities of the librarian operating the current system. Many of the problems of initiating changes based on modern technology, may in fact be circumvented by deciding that the new information system is a "res sui generis", and not appropriate for nesting within the existing institutions or library structures. In this use, staff can be selected specifically to match the requirements of the new function, who will have a strong incentive for making the new system work. This avoids the problems inherent in trying to modify existing structures against the resistance of veteran staff with a vested interest in maintaining the status quo. Shifts of status and in the lines of communication, entailed by change, tend to be traumatic for all concerned. The identical reasons justify training and education in "information science" to be distinguished as a separate academic discipline, different from "library service" and other established schools.

### 6.2.2. Modifying an existing system

This is the approach most commonly used, where each function perceives of applications of computer techniques which appear beneficial. A charging system is developed for the library, a payroll system for the accountant, inventory control and personnel systems for other functions. Thus a patchwork of systems is developed where each should have been conceived as a subsystem of the whole system. The user who has to interface with several of these separate services is compelled to learn many unrelated systems. The problems of preparing staff for acceptance of change have been discussed above in relation to the subject of system dynamics.

### 6.2.3. Integration of new capabilities into overall organizations

In this approach an in-depth study of the organization that the information system is serving, of the available inputs and desired outputs is made from the viewpoint of optimizing the function of the global organization. Such an approach should be triggered within senior management when it is asked to finance introduction of computer techniques into any of its subsystems. The first requirement will be to define the use of information in relation to the objectives of the organization (see Chapter 3—Planning). Then the sources and channels of information must be reviewed in terms of the hierarchy of decision-makers. In short, needs of the users of the system must balance Phasing-out of the old against Phasing-in of the new system.

## 6.3. Problem areas

The problems associated with the dynamics of a changing system discussed earlier for individuals, often apply in an exacerbated degree when the participating persons are corporate entities. Positions are taken up which do not allow for an orderly retreat. The consequences of a rigid stance may be much more unfavorable than if some degree of accommodation or compromise is accepted. In most cases, policy is set at a high level but most negotiations are conducted at lower levels where no flexibility is permissible in interpreting corporate policy.

Because of semantic confusion, authority which has been validly exercised in one area, is extrapolated into areas which seemingly are closely related, but which may require new levels and kinds of expertise, requiring years in the acquisition. This problem has often arisen in the information field, largely because of improper definition of terms commonly used, and because the field appears very attractive to those anxious for added responsibility and status as indicated above. Terms, the misuse of which has given rise to serious consequences, include: information, systems analysis, communications, management information systems.

The term "information" must always be interpreted in context of the person using the term. Information, as defined in signal transmission theory following Shannon, is an abstract concept, equated with negentropy. This definition is followed by communications engineers, who find it a convenient basis for the measurement of "information"-carrying capacity of communication channels.

Information, in the view of the manager of a computer center, is equated with data, and the terms "information processing" and "data processing" are used as if they were interchangeable.

The librarian often feels that he is above all a supplier of information and that the operation of information centers, even of information analysis centers, is a natural extension of his domain. In reality, he has traditionally been concerned rather with the packages which contain information (books, journals etc.) rather than with the information content of these packages, and with the passive archiving function rather than the active function of dissemination. The extension, in practice, from a library to an information analysis center, involves a quantum jump in expertise relating to the subject-content of the material disseminated by the center, and the transition has often been painful (Rees, 1972).

The fact that the movement of information within networks, invokes use of communications facilities, that is, calls another class of organization onto the picture. Because of the high technical sophistication (and cost) of modern telecommunications, arguments could even be mounted for administration of information systems by the communications experts just as well as by any of the entities situated at individual nodes of the total information network. In many cases the ultimate user/supplier community may be the most appropriate party for the control of information.

Because computing operations were originally most closely associated with the accounting function, there is even a tendency in many cases, for any activity which involves considerable computer processing, to come under the authority of agencies whose prime responsibility is the control of the flow of funds or just government bureaucracy. This can become hazardous to the individual, "the little man", the ultimate user/supplier of information.

In individual organizations, the administrative location of an information center is likely to have any of the associations enumerated above, largely dependent on the entrepreneurial character of the persons who sparked formation of the center.

A study of the problem of effectively managing and disseminating information, immediately compels the conclusion that economies of operation are closely related to size, and that the problems of ensuring compatibility between autonomous systems may well be insurmountable. This leads to the concept of total integration of control and operation. There is a tendency for strong organizations, already peripherally in the general field of handling information, to attempt to preempt a dominant role in the development of supraorganizational information systems. In many cases, there are several such bodies of approximately equal status and the prime result is to postpone implementation of an overall system.

### 6.3.1. Problems of total system integration

In viewing a proposed overall system, the occurrence of computer elements has usually dominated the thinking of people concerned with development or operation of the proposed system (Saracevic, 1971). Actually, very few of the potential users of a system are capable of directly using the type of information available from the system, whether it be computer printout, technical reports, or bibliographic references available at a terminal. The definition of the problem giving rise to the need for information, is itself much more difficult than problems in accessing the system. For most people there is an absolute need for a human intermediary between the man with the problem, and the machine. The computer because of its great speed in meticulously sorting through digitized data, can augment the capabilities of the intermediary, but generally it is the latter who is the key element in the system. Thus, if effective arguments are to be made in support of a centralized system, they must not be based solely on the potential economies of scale in use of machines and buildings, but on the capability of providing a sufficient spectrum of subject experts to aid users of the system. There is evidently little justification for assuming that these subject experts should be subordinate to the management of the machine, which is merely another element of the overall system.

Effective administration of very large man-machine systems, in which the human element consists of highly skilled professional, rather than clerical staff, has not yet been successfully demonstrated. Only in those cases where the function of the human has been quite stereotyped, as in airline reservations systems, or switchboard services, has some success been recorded. Even there in some cases where a higher level of sophistication has been sought, disastrous failures have occurred. Thus a major argument against attempting to forge a single entity with complete authority in the area of information dissemination, is the fact that it is very difficult to operate such an organization. To attempt this solution is courting failure on the grand scale. This is particularly the case if the proposed entity can only be built by dismantling established and successful subsystems.

### 6.3.2. Problems of distributed system structures

As the limits on the contribution that machine technology can make to information dissemination become more fully realized, it will become obvious that the human elements are still the most important part of an information system. The analysis and evaluation of information are the prerogative of humans, not of machines. In the most successful centers, such as those operated by the Battelle Institute, it is found that the people operating the system, must continue to be active in their normal research and development activities. Translation full-time into a library-type environment rapidly blunts the edge of their expertise and voids their authority as experts among their peers. It is evident that a monolithic body, aimed at covering all subject-areas, could not surround itself with sufficiently complete laboratory and design facilities, to fulfil these requirements. In addition, the formation of megaliths of this type has a stultifying effect on its staff and inevitably substitutes administrative for creative ability as measures of achievement (Haggerty, 1969).

The division of labor according to capability leads to the concept of smaller, entrepreneurial centers which are relatively more effective in research and development than larger organizations. If the staffing is adequate to maintain momentum beyond the "take-off" requirement, the scientists and engineers will in furtherance of their own goals, maintain full awareness of progress in their own field, and inevitably form a suitable cadre of experts capable of information analysis in depth.

Technical aspects of information retrieval are sometimes favored by use of centers of excellence as host organization. In an all-encompassing system, indexing necessarily is often more general in nature than is desirable for precision in retrieval. This is largely because of the difficulty in achieving consistency in indexing when many indexers are involved, and partly because it is not practical to have a sufficient number of specialist indexers to cover every facet of a subject. At autonomous specialist centers, microthesauri can be used to provide indexing in depth. Expertise in indexing is ensured in some cases by enlisting the cooperation of scientists active in the specialist fields.

When a flexible and dynamic structure based on a number of autonomous subsystems is sought, problems of compatibility of query systems, database and of indexing, can arise. In the next section we shall consider these problems for systems which touch or overlap.

### 6.3.3. Problems of participation and feedback

A vital element in planning of any system which will impinge on many organizations and individuals is that of ensuring participation of users of the system and operators of subsystems, in the planning process. Mechanisms based on users' groups and specialist committees help in some measure, but in reality it is difficult to give a voice to all those who have a valid interest in the development. Furthermore, professionals active in the field of systems development are initially the only ones who have a full understanding of the state-of-the-art capabilities and of significant technological developments approaching fruition. However, this should not be made an excuse to allow the deliberations of the "wise men" responsible for system planning to be shrouded in secrecy and mystery. There is still a considerable current of distaste among people generally, with respect to computers and information systems, which they feel might be used to spy or otherwise clandestinely monitor private aspects of men's lives. This fear might not perhaps be relevant to the case of data bases containing only bibliographic citations (though even these are now being used for mechanical evaluation of research productivity). It certainly has some relevance to systems containing general statistics about the population, which are used by firms for market surveys, or in the recording of applications for support of research and development, etc.

Aside from problems of privacy relating to data banks, all those who have a vested interest in maintaining or promoting existing information systems will assume the worst if they are excluded for long stretches of time, from secret discussions on the future of their systems. The wise planner will want continuous feedback... a dialogue... with the users and operators as his plans evolve and gell.

# CHAPTER 7

# Information Systems for Administrative Decision Making

The success of any system can only be measured in terms of the satisfaction of the user. The prime use of information is to provide a basis for decisions. Thus it is appropriate to attempt an in-depth analysis of the user as decision-maker.

Advanced techniques of communication, computers and audiovisual aids have been extensively used to eliminate the drudgery from many business activities and provide economies in jobs where much clerical help was needed. Systems known as Management Information Systems (MIS), provide means for documenting the trivia of business activities and for generating summary statistical reports to aid the middle manager in monitoring these activities. However, the full potential of modern devices for augmenting human skills has not been realized due to the inadequate integration of these techniques, each excellent in itself. The many operational systems have at present only one common element—the man who makes use of them. He must learn to use each system on an individual basis. Complete integration, correlation, and synthesis occur in his mind, rather than in a system feeding information to him.

Surely a level of sophistication has now been reached

where a preliminary synthesis of these many elements can be achieved with the aid of computers. The final coordination and evaluation of the integrated data must still remain the responsibility of the man, but much of the redundancy can be eliminated and detailed processing can be carried out more rapidly and accurately with the aid of machines of various types.

Man, who is the target (a node in an information network, Fig. 4) of converging streams of information, must make decisions based on the data received and transmit this information to the network. For the purposes of this book, the user is considered not only as an isolated individual but as an element in some large organization as well. The organization is assumed to have some idealized pyramidal structure (a hierarchy) of the line-and-staff type. Neither the exact type of organization, whether commercial or governmental, nor its size will have much effect on the general analysis.

It is to be expected that full utilization of mind-augmenting resources already available will not be achieved without reconfiguring organization structures and modifying personal habits to harmonize with the new possibilities. The concept of congregating workers into large groups is not consonant with proper use of communications techniques that effectively annul space and time between people situated at different locations. The depth of hierarchical structures, as well as the relative importance of lateral or vertical flow of authority will probably have to be modified to optimize integrated decision-making (management) systems (DMS) containing advanced machine elements. Thus final achievement of such a goal would certainly take a decade of effort.

## 7.1. Communication hierarchies and interfaces

Communication within an organization, or between it and other organizations, calls for the making of decisions accord-

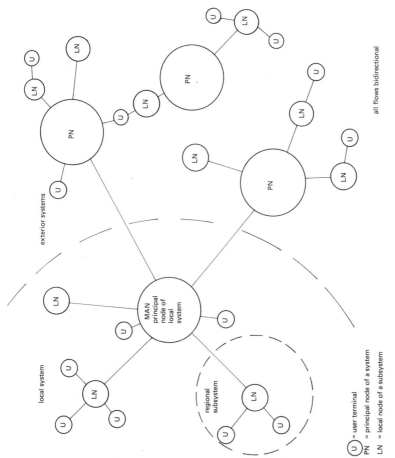

FIG. 4. Information network (schematic).

ing to the status of the individuals involved within the respective hierarchies. At the lowest level, the individual carries out tasks in reaction to instructions received and need make few decisions requiring significant amounts of information beyond the rules of the procedure manual defining his task. His time-span for response to a requirement is very short and he normally cannot initiate communication with others, except in the form of routine data-entry in a rigid format. This is an example of *operative information.*

At the top of the hierarchy, the individual is not often in the position of having to react to exogenous events. He originates *directive information* which may affect all lower-ranking members of the organization and he makes all essential policy decisions. The time-span of such activities is long and he is concerned mainly with the future and with setting the style of the organization. On the other hand, at crisis times he must make decisions rapidly. In both of these modes of action, as planner or prime decision-maker, he needs to call on a large body of information, which has been predigested according to rules which he recognizes, principally by mobilizing his staff officers. Broad policy developed by the top manager forms a directive basis for operative information and rules to be formulated by middle managers to govern day-to-day operations (Langefors, 1973).

Middle management is primarily concerned with day-to-day management of ongoing activities, and with implementing the policies initiated by top management. He ensures orderly replacement of resources used and monitors the flow of activities of the staff within his functional area. His time-span is intermediate between those of the other two classes described and he operates primarily from endogenous information as provided by a conventional MIS.

Staff-officers, not directly within the chain of authority of a line-type structure, are not primarily decision-makers so much as transducers and evaluators of information which can influence current and future policies and operations of the organization. They provide technical advice to top and middle management to assist in integration of the total activities of the organization with a view to optimizing the overall system and identifying new opportunities. They must be particularly sensitive to change outside the organization which requires continuous adaptation of the local system to ensure continuing viability. They have the longest time-span for activities of the classes noted, and the greatest need for exogenous and endogenous information. The essential problem is that of matching channels of communication to the category of user of an information system (Amey, 1968).

A conclusion may immediately be drawn as to the place of computer aids in such a system. There is a hierarchy of media suitable for the presentation of information related to the hierarchy of decision-makers. Direct communication with a computer, at present, requires keying of queries or data. It is thus unlikely that at the current state-of-the art, where direct voice communication in natural language with a computer, capable of inferential analysis, has not been achieved in a working system, that top management can make direct use of computer aids. There are some tasks for which humans will be superior to computers for at least the next twenty years (Dreyfus, 1972) and a new class of staff officers, information-aides (see page 65, Training of Information Aides) will be needed in this transition period as an interface between people and specialized information sources. Visual aids, whether to display analogue or other data stored in a data-bank, or for use in video-conferences, may soon be used.

At middle-management levels, conventional management information systems (MIS) process and digest internally generated (endogenous) data to document the movement of people or material within the organization (personnel records and logistics), provide accounting aids and even make decisions (reorder time and quantity for stores) according to algorithms designed by technical staff and authorized by higher management. Better use of the data in these systems may even enable emerging problems to be foreseen before the crisis point is reached, and possible solutions to be formulated by the computer. In fact several of the decisions formerly requiring human intervention may soon be replaced by automatic computer response based on algorithms which are a concrete expression of top management policy. The skills of middle managers will be needed primarily in formulating these algorithms and coping with exceptions not provided for in the programs (bugs).

At lower operational levels data will continue to be entered by traditional keying methods. There will be an increase in task-scheduling and prompting by programmed computers. Simple interactions with the system will continue to be mediated by codes rather than by natural language, or by simple voice or light-pen type response to multiple choices offered by voice or visual displays.

## 7.2. Management information systems (MIS)

MIS were developed to monitor everyday operations of organizations by processing clerical data and digital or analog inputs from automated processes imbedded in the work stream, related to routine transactions of strictly defined types, and are now at a quite mature state of development. A high level of integration of subsystems such as pay, logistics, personnel data, etc. into corporate data-bases, has been achieved. Statistical reports are generated automatically or on command by standardized report generators. Quick response can be provided when required for individual transactions. The logic of these systems often requires that large-scale computers be used to manipulate large data-bases depending on the nature of the application. If the complexity of processing is not too great (i.e., only a limited number of tightly defined queries is allowed) many users can be serviced, as in the case of various reservations systems, e.g., for airlines. To date, attempts to combine complex processing with fast response systems for many users, have not been successful.

### 7.3. Information storage and retrieval systems (IS&R)

Information-retrieval systems, such as those used in library or scientific documentation activities, are conceptually at a high level of development. The more sophisticated types provide immediate response to queries to enable the user to redefine his requirements in the light of the data he receives. Large data-bases are required with greater flexibility of definition than is usually allowed in MIS or the reservation systems of airlines. The complexity of file-handling and processing is usually such that a dedicated computer system is required, even to handle a relatively small number of users. An IS&R system differs from the MIS in that some of the data may be stored in more than one file in the system to facilitate speed of searching and ensure adequately fast response to online queries.

Where as data in a MIS is usually endogenous, the bulk of data in an IS&R system is exogenous. Even the largest system of the latter type could not possibly hold, online, all the information that a user might wish to search. Thus complex selection and purging techniques must be employed to ensure that only the most frequently used material is stored in the local, rapid-access files. Since complete control of all information that may be needed is not possible, coordination of the internal system with external ones is needed to make fullest use of all available information. In most disciplines, any one nation, such as Canada or Sweden, generates only a few percent of the current production of new knowledge. The contribution to the total cumulated stores of information is even smaller. Information from many external systems may well be required by a user normally served by a specialized system. It would be unfeasible to attempt to create a single giant system (a megalith) which is supposed to combine all data into one exhaustive data-base, serviced by a single vast computer (Riley, 1971).

Reorganization of data in a MIS within an IS&R system could be worthwhile to determine implicit correlations, e.g., between personnel movements and material wastage; or between incidence of illness and geographical location—which would not be apparent in a conventional MIS. In other words the original management information system (MIS) had better be designed in such a way that future desirable uses of the existing information can be anticipated. In practice this means that exploiting the flexibility of multiple files often necessitates that a generalized file handling or database management system be developed to support the MIS and IS&R systems for swift retrieval.

## 7.4. Administrative information systems—The office

Up till the present, an area where computer-based techniques have made little impact is that of office-activity. The principal methods of communication for administrative purposes are conversation in person or by telephone with other people and correspondence by mail or memos. The organization of mail is in essence a library process. Incoming mail is date-stamped, logged, classified by subject, entered into a file-cover and circulated to the addressee or a number of individuals who might be interested, or responsible for taking action on it. The addressee writes a reply, a copy of which is filed with the original letter or transaction form.

In this case, file-handling entails loss of file-integrity whenever some of the dossiers are in the hands of individuals. Since the file-cover hopefully contains all relevant documents on the subject, only one person can deal with this subject at a time if duplicate copies are not made. In practice, duplicates of part of the master file are maintained in the office files of individuals. These occupy considerable space and individual dossiers are never as complete or up to date as those in the central file ought to be.

Application of modern techniques has been made to one variety of incoming mail, to wit, that received by telegraph. In the system designed by IT&T for the US State Department, telegraph signals (i.e., messages in machine-readable form) are displayed on cathode ray tubes (CRT) for assessment by message analysts. On the basis of content, the latter determine a list of individuals to whom the message should be circulated for comment or action. The messages are then reproduced in the required numbers of copies and transmitted to recipients by internal office-mail. The message itself is stored in a data-bank which can be queried from terminals.

This system appears to have a gross drawback in that it multiplies the amount of paper stored. It would appear preferable if terminals with CRT displays were provided for all recipients who could then be signalled whenever a message had been routed to them for action. The officer could press a key causing the message to be displayed and immediately enter his comments or route the message to others. No paper need enter into the transaction. SDI (Selective Dissemination of Information) of messages would continue to an individual only until a response had been formulated at which time it would be too late for him to make a significant contribution.

Such an approach appears to be the way of the future when mailing of paper will most certainly be replaced by electromagnetically transmitted signals.

In the transition period during which typewritten correspondence will remain the norm, machine-readable data can be provided as a byproduct of typing, either at an edited terminal such as those of the IBM ATS system (Administrative Terminal System) or by sufficiently standardizing type-face quality of paper and typewriter ribbon and letter-format so that Optical Character Recognition (OCR) systems can be used to capture all or part of the typed material.

### 7.4.1. Indexing of transactions for filing

The greatest weakness of traditional filing methods is in indexing. Items are usually filed uniquely under a single subject heading and are thus difficult to retrieve. This method is similar to that of shelving books according to subject in a conventional library. However, libraries usually have catalog cards to provide cross-referencing and multiple entries. This is not customary in a filing system for transactions, internal memos, external messages or correspondence, even in a well managed library. An integrative approach should be used even though an overall integrated information system may not be within immediate reach for libraries, archives or other organizations.

If the item were to be filed under more than one heading, it would need to be duplicated in order to provide other copies held in other file-covers. This leads to difficulties in keeping the files updated.

The first requirement for an efficient system is to divorce the physical location of an item from subject-dependence. Filing of incoming documents or transactions at one node of a network, should be in strict chronological order of receipt. Ancillary files (which could be card files in the interim stage of changing over to a machine-system) will then locate the accession number according to subject, date of receipt, etc. Minimum indexing requires that codes for sender, recipient and subject should be entered on each piece of a transaction as it is entered into the sequential file (which may be in microform, after a photoreduction operation).

Indexing is currently done by clerical help. The quality should be upgraded by the addition of more subject entries and better definition of indexing terms used. Mnemonic or other codes, authorized by a standard codebook must be used for entering data that identifies the source and recipient of the letter. Accessions of memoranda, etc. received from sources endogenous to the system (or cooperating with it) could be coded at source, reinforcing the intent of the sender.

If such subject, source and recipient files are entered into a computerized data-bank, machine-edits can be used to ensure that valid codes are used, and thus make retrieval at a later date much easier.

## 7.4.2. Retrieval of filed transactions

When an individual has been actively working on a task for some time, he will usually know exactly which files are of most use to him. Another person, tackling the problem for the first time, is not in so fortunate a position. Since report or letter writers do not always treat one subject per document item, relevant data may very well be contained in dossiers, the main subject heading of which appears to be very different from the target subject.

Complete analytic cataloguing by a transaction- or document-analyst can solve this problem, but it is a very expensive undertaking and tends to delay handling of the file and thus action on the messages received. In addition, it is not always possible to predict how the information in the file may be used in the future. Thus indexing that is adequate for current requirements may rapidly obsolesce.

If the messages are received in machine-readable form, they can be indexed by computer, using conventional methods. In addition, if it is desired to search an old file recorded in this manner, it is relatively simple to reindex the material for searching according to the concepts then current.

When transactions are received from an external organization, it is evidently difficult to impose on the generators of exogenous data the requirement that their documents and messages be in machine-readable form. Thus machine indexing of incoming material will not be practical in the near future without expensive re-keying. However, practically all messages are tightly linked to other messages generated within the organization for which machine indexing is feasible, usually by the subject code (currently called file reference number). In searching a file this citation coupling can be used to transfer, in effect, the indexing of the endogenous data (outgoing correspondence) to the exogenous data (incoming mail). The method suggested is analogous to bibliographic coupling as exploited in services such as the Citation Index (Garfield, 1964). Once an organization such as a library adopts the principle of automation, the full benefits of efficient computer usage should be taken into account, especially for "simple" and clerical tasks as described above.

### 7.4.3. Integration of administrative information services

By use of a universal query language, to be proposed below, it is possible to tap sources of information from many autonomous systems specializing in their own areas of excellence. These may be:

(a) Information retrieval systems of RECON type (NASA, 1970),
(b) MIS data banks,
(c) stored drawings,
(d) stored correspondence,
(e) personal files.

Television-type displays should preferably be used where graphics are to be exhibited. Since both video and digital data need to be displayed, either two terminals may be used or one terminal with a split screen.

Actual modification in real time of designs using a cursor or light pen should properly be done at a special terminal, rather than at the general purpose split-screen type noted above.

In addition to retrieval services, communication between user terminals should be possible, as in current APL systems, with controlled sharing of user files.

Other possible uses are of the Day-timer variety:

(a) recording appointments,
(b) tickler reminder systems,
(c) daily planner and organizer, etc.

Reminders of appointments could be routed automatically by computer through, for instance, the Bell telephone system, using synthesized voice messages, to officers at conferences or on business trips if desired, or voice data transmitted in response to prearranged codes using touchtone telephone.

Selective Dissemination of Information, with time-limits for response to action notes, can also be incorporated into the system to aid in integration of responses to messages received.

The ability to modify certain files, under full access control, is important in areas of high technical content, where specific experts in a field may be given authority to change or add to indexing of technical data, and add numerical data or review material to analytic cataloguing data provided by the basic manual or machine system via a "wait" file. Thus information analysis activities can be carried out by those most competent to do so from their own office or laboratory.

In a fully integrated system, the principal means of communication is via the computer-system. That is, everyone, down to the lowliest staff member would have a terminal of some kind. The inventory-clerk may work with a T-scan type, the typist will require a full keyboard, with upper-and-lower case displayed on the screen. Terminals capable of multicoloured displays of graphics will be required at the higher levels. The cost of such terminals should within five years drop to no more than $1000 per basic CRT terminal with upper and lower case characters. Videophone facilities will be required in conference rooms to avoid unnecessary travelling to attend business meetings. The inputs and display must be convenient, and acceptable to the level of user for which they are designed. Human engineering is essential to avoid user frustration. The system must be a forgiving one and have acceptable default options when the user does not address it in an optimum manner (Amey, 1970).

### 7.4.4. Elements of an integrated administrative system

*Traffic density.* Certain activities are so specialized in nature that they are most appropriately treated as autonomous subsystems; e.g., information services serving design centres or research establishments working in highly specialized subject areas. Since the traffic associated with these databases is concentrated at nodes sited at appropriate centres of specialization, it is not cost-effective to maintain the same data at some central node with its prime dedication to general use. Online, reactive (fast-response) querying is usually required of large dedicated disc-files. The principal output activity of these files will be stimulated by the information specialists responsible for analyzing and searching this data. Thus needless cost would be incurred in communication between the central computer and the terminals of the information specialists if all traffic is routed through the centre. Needless processing overheads will be incurred by combining this specialized information system with others of unrelated type.

A similar analysis applies to processing of data relating to administrative detail at local centres. For example, in the military control and planning in ordering provisions for consumption at local messes is most appropriately carried out on a day-to-day basis by an autonomous subsystem. Only report information from digested data on gross movement of funds and supplies need be periodically passed to the central node of the information system.

The existence of natural nodes in a network of communicating computers can be detected by a traffic analysis of messages circulating in the system. Cost-effectiveness indicates that heavy local traffic should be switched, controlled and recorded at a local node (Riley, 1971).

*Interfacing nodes.* Special consideration must be given to ensure that the master node will be able to communicate with and monitor local nodes. This calls for a certain degree of standardization:

(a) Between data-elements common to the MIS and the subsystem.

(b) Formats and codes for interchange of information between autonomous subsystems having data-elements not part of the MIS for tape or line transmission.

(c) The query-language for querying files serviced at any node within the system (irrespective of local file-structures).

(d) Coordination of system planning with external organizations which will be called upon frequently to supply specialist information, exogenous to the organization. Use of a common methodology is desirable for meaningful communication between system managers.

## 7.5. Evolution of an administrative information system

Conceptual studies of formal elements of a system are necessary to ensure that elements which are being developed independently will mesh to form parts of the optimal total plan. This will allow for orderly progression from the original hybrid collection of uncoordinated subsystems, which entail much duplication of file-storage and overlapping of file-handling activities, to an integrated overall system, with fast response and minimum duplication of files or effort. Formal analysis of the essential parameters of the system will allow standardization of those parameters which will continue to be used, perhaps stored and processed in different ways, throughout the evolution of the system.

### 7.5.1. Man–machine integration

*Human problems arising during system development.* The introduction of computers into operations, formerly carried out by other means, has usually resulted in frustration and opposition from the people operating the system undergoing change. Proper use of computers appears to require a fundamental reorganization of the managerial structure of an organization, initially with some individuals losing status or freedom of action, as a result. Thus a revolution in the way administration is carried on, inevitably will call forth resistance which can easily destroy the cost effectiveness of the changes. This is most apparent where incumbents of critical positions have held the same post for many years. Needless to say the problems are not all generated by the staff of the manual system who probably are doing an excellent job using the traditional approach. System analysts occasionally take simplistic views of operations and tend to find neat solutions for watered down versions of the operation which omit all the virtues of the system being superseded (Amey, 1970).

Re-education of staff to new ways may be impossible, especially if they are unwilling to cooperate. In organizations where postings are not of long duration, the problem can be less abrasive since phasing-in of a new mode of operation can be synchronized with transfer of staff who might otherwise prove to be obstacles to successful implementation of the plan. Change, when properly handled, can even result in improved morale of the workers involved, as in the well-known Hawthorne effect.

The importance of people in the overall system must never be minimized. The system is not an end in itself. It is intended to augment the capability of its human masters. Machine-efficiency should be subordinated to the comfort and convenience of system users. As the cost of hardware continuously decreases, it becomes evident that the main costs of a total system will continue to be the salaries of the human components.

### 7.5.2. Milestones of implementation

Milestones of implementation can be planned to ensure that independent elements of the final system can be implemented in stages which achieve quantum jumps in efficiency and convenience due to carrying out the plan. A system which demands extra effort and a change in the habits of the people involved, without any apparent increase in convenience or status for the participants, is unlikely to succeed. Implementation should be attempted initially only for part of the organization, while the bugs are being removed.

### 7.5.3. Model elements and pilot networks

Implementation within the planning group itself if possible, would be the logical first step, since its members should have a vested interest in getting the system to work. In operating realistic models of the final system, the essential character of the inputs and outputs (format, response time, display mode, human-machine interface etc.) should appear the same as in the target system. Ideally the new services should sell themselves so that the potential users will request that the system be extended to them. It is evident that the specific hardware configuration used during this stage need not be that chosen for final implementation. It should be close enough so as not to affect credibility of applicability of the simulator.

### 7.5.4. Program initiation

In an evolutionary approach such as that sketched in Chapter 6, several items can be singled out for immediate action in a multi-pronged approach to the problem.

*Information services* have already been developed to service many activities. However, clerical transaction handling has not registered much impact from the introduction of computers into the conduct of business. Thus the subsystem dealing with automatic filing, indexing and display of correspondence deserves special attention. The precise modalities used—whether digitally-indexed video-tapes (e.g. Ampex and Sony systems) or microfilms—is not important during the stage in which the mode of retrieval and display to the user is being developed. Such a system should be implemented on a realistic scale, as soon as possible, to enable conceptual bugs to be ironed out. The main requirement is for flexibility so that continual enhancement is possible based on feedback from a sample population of real users. Provision for automatic feedback of user response should be incorporated in the system ab initio.

*Indexing standards* are needed for transactions and other files where these are not currently available or adequate. Coding of the sources of correspondence is an essential requirement to facilitate retrieval of stored information. From the beginning, a method must be incorporated for validating source codes; for updating source codes as names of organizations change; and for linking of files relating to both old and new names. Tracing name-changes in old files is one of the most time-consuming of clerical tasks.

*Traffic analysis* of existing correspondence, signals and other communications within and beyond the organization is necessary to determine the optimal size for data-processing operating elements. Perhaps, in the early stages, the more refined processing should apply only to correspondence and other information traffic between managers in higher echelons of the organization. The direction of flow of communication and the receipt-response loops for messages should indicate the most cost-effective application of DP equipment.

*Query language.* For internal efficiency, subsystems will need to operate in modes internally optimized for the specific subsystem. Complete integration of different modes of operation appears to be impractical and uneconomic. However, portions of the data, digested and evaluated locally, may be required to contribute data-elements to the central system. If the data in a subsystem is to be queried directly, by any user in the overall system (possibly switched through the central computing node), it is necessary to define a system-wide query language which with default options, can be used to query any accessible file within the system. Otherwise it would be necessary for each user to know the job control language and local query language of each of the subsystems. Definition of this language should commence at an early stage since it is certain to have an impact on the file-structures and manipulation capabilities of each of the subsystems. Where desired, the subsystem could provide an interpretative front-end to allow for translation of a standard query into the format required for the local system.

*Training of information aides.* It is possible that the final information system will take over many of the secretary's tasks. However, making use of the complete range of information services that will be available at various stages of development, will require skilled technical help to interface between the senior decision-maker and the system. Acceptance by users of radical changes in doing business by the methods sketched, calls for accurate delineation of this function and training of information aides (special staff officers) at a very early stage of the development. This is all the more important as the system will be in constant flux for many years as each subsystem is brought online and separately debugged. The essential role of this class of staff cannot be too strongly emphasized. It is analogous to the role of the service engineer supplied by major hardware suppliers to help introduce a computer and maintain it for a client.

*Prototype operations* already exist that include many of the functions and features described above. Most advanced is NLS developed by the Augmented Knowledge Workshop at SRI and designed by Engelbart (1973).

# CHAPTER 8

# *Problems of Compatibility and Coordination*

Problems arise in transferring information into, within and out of an information system, and each of the system interfaces. The main areas in which these problems arise will be discussed under the following headings:

Documents,
Surrogates and indexing,
Communications,
Input–output devices and formats,
Computer processing.

The solution to these problems is to develop a metasystem as the logical matrix within which the specific subsystems operate. When interrogating his own subsystem, the user need not be aware of the existence of a metastructure and can use the local query language. Links with other autonomous subsystems will however be via commands belonging to the meta operating language and the common query language. Each subsystem must have a front end capable of accepting a minimal subset of the commands and queries from the metasystem.

## 8.1. Documents

Documents are essentially the packages of full-text material and may be in the form of printed matter, magnetic tapes, microforms, videodata, etc. indexed by digital data. Differences of textual language give rise to problems in indexing and comprehension. It is still considered unlikely that adequate machine-translation will be available by 1980. Unstandardized type-faces, scripts and formats makes machine conversion (optical reading) from printed to machine-readable form very expensive if even possible. Hand-written material such as is standard in Urdu publications will not be machine-processable before the problem of machine-translation is solved. The problems are related since they are both essentially problems of pattern recognition, which up till now only the human brain can solve sufficiently.

## 8.2. Surrogates and indexing

Surrogates are documents or messages used to describe summarily and thus take the place of the complete text or document; viz. catalogue cards, abstract collections whether printed or in machine-readable form. The bibliographic items to be used must be defined preferably as a subset of a universal list.

If indexing of a document is not derived automatically by computer from the natural language of the document, then the problem of incompatibility of thesauri arises. General thesauri such as the TEST thesaurus, developed by the US Engineering Joint Council, are not considered adequate to distinguish items in any highly specialized field. The only possible solution is use of a microthesaurus which is a subset of the metathesaurus of the global system. The metathesaurus or classification could have numerical code representation (e.g., UDC), so as not to favour any one language or script.

## 8.3. Communications

Compatibility problems in coding systems, signal levels etc. between computer and common carrier have been solved for all major computer models. The type of output available is determined by the type of line used. Subvoice grade allows only typewriter output, voice of printer output and broadband of fast displays via a cathode ray tube. Keys and other codes used for maintaining privacy must obviously be particularized within the subsystem. The metasystem would have its own access controls for switching between subsystems.

## 8.4. Input–output devices and formats

Standards are being developed to cover problems in this area. The interface between a subsystem and the metasystem should be capable of communicating between the minimal terminal device, defined for the entire system, and the particular subsystem.

## 8.5. Computer processing

A search program written in the assembly language of one computer will not generally run on another. Advances in techniques of microprogramming are simplifying the problem of transportability of programs. However, in an information network it is more practical to leave the full freedom of programming with the operators of subsystems. A front end needs to be provided at each subsystem interface, which interprets queries originating with the metasystem, into the local language, leaving the mechanism transparent to the user.

## 8.6. Compatibility and the metasystem

The design of the metasystem can be elaborated to the point where it can translate any consistent set of data or codes into another. However, even the most diverse of systems have some elements in common. Personnel systems have people's names, as do bibliographic data systems. Geographical place names are common to land inventory systems as well as many others. It is evident that universal formats and coding of contact elements of this type should be agreed on by all subsystems of the global system. Alternatively, but at higher cost, the elements of a metasystem which provide interfacing with the overall system, can carry out the task. Dictionaries of contact-elements in the metalanguage of the total system are therefore necessary. Many of the problems of interfacing diverse computer systems are now being solved by the ARPANET project (Carr et al., 1970).

The only point at which a user need be aware of the metasystem occurs when he wishes to query a databank other than his local databank. In this case, instead of using the query language of the local subsystem, he must use the common query language of the larger system. Each subsystem contributing to the overall system will be required to be able to respond to a minimal subset of the common query language. Descriptors, item identifiers, corporate names etc. will be subsets of the metalanguage of the overall system when querying in this mode. The metalanguage will comprise all contact elements which provide commonality within the system. As mentioned earlier (Section 3.3.1), every system is part of a still larger system. This circumstance calls for the crude definition of certain meta-levels and metasystems as we proceed toward the development and growth of information networks internationally.

CHAPTER 9

# Networks and Structuring

It appears that the present decade of the 1970's will be characterized by general international movements toward the development of networks for information activities. In agreement with our introductory definitions (Section 1.2) we might have a general information system depicted as Fig. 5. Analogously we may use the following network definition:

*Network* is a distribution system composed of interlinked, spatially dispersed channels, subsystems and/or elements; but not all systems are networks i.e. the systems do not always have meshs or coils.

Traditionally, the most familiar cases of networks are railroads and airline traffic routes at the macro level, or circulatory and neural nets at the micro level. Those networks are often characterized by some kind of dynamic flow. Other networks may be of static nature, such as thesauri, cognitive maps, corporate organization charts, planning networks etc. Administrative networks were covered in Chapters 7 and 8.

The step-by-step development of international information systems covers all stages of macro-macro, macro-micro and micro-micro networks. The most cumbersome and costly efforts are required with respect to the macro-macro networks. We shall therefore elaborate on these issues in particular.

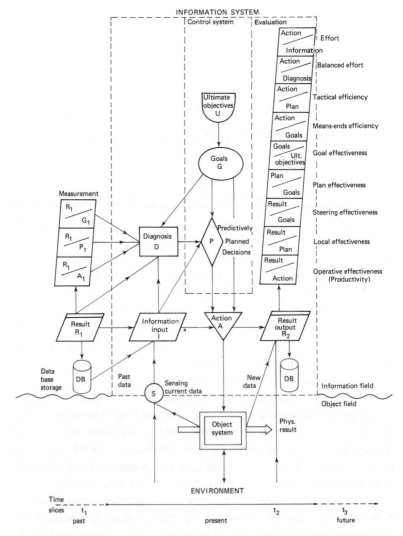

FIG. 5. General information system structure (existing feedback loops not shown).

Several international, macro-level networks can be distinguished, the most important of which are:

(a) Information networks,
(b) Communication networks,
(c) Computer networks,
(d) Relational networks,
(e) Network hybrids.

Although the development toward international networks is cumbersome, the need is based on well founded reasons such as:

(a) closing the loops toward bidirectional communication;
(b) closing the gaps between isolated elements or potential subsystems;
(c) sharing of resources, costs and maintenance;
(d) decentralized distribution of facilities and service points;
(e) increasing reliability, fall-back and safety;
(f) diminishing the loss of time and energy;
(g) double or multiple operations for mutual comparison of gained experience;
(h) balance of control.

The preliminary structuring of networks should be exercised as a systems analyst's job of modelling and initial planning before pilot projects or testbed operations are to be undertaken. There exist a manifold of typical networks structures, that have been studied and are described in the open literature (Borko, 1972, Samuelson, 1971b). The evolutionary morphology of network structures is a significant example of how experience and growth trends can be taken account of while utilizing system analysis as a means of predictive planning (Fig. 6). Just as a plant or a garden can only be grown in certain ways, there exist specific empiric mechan-

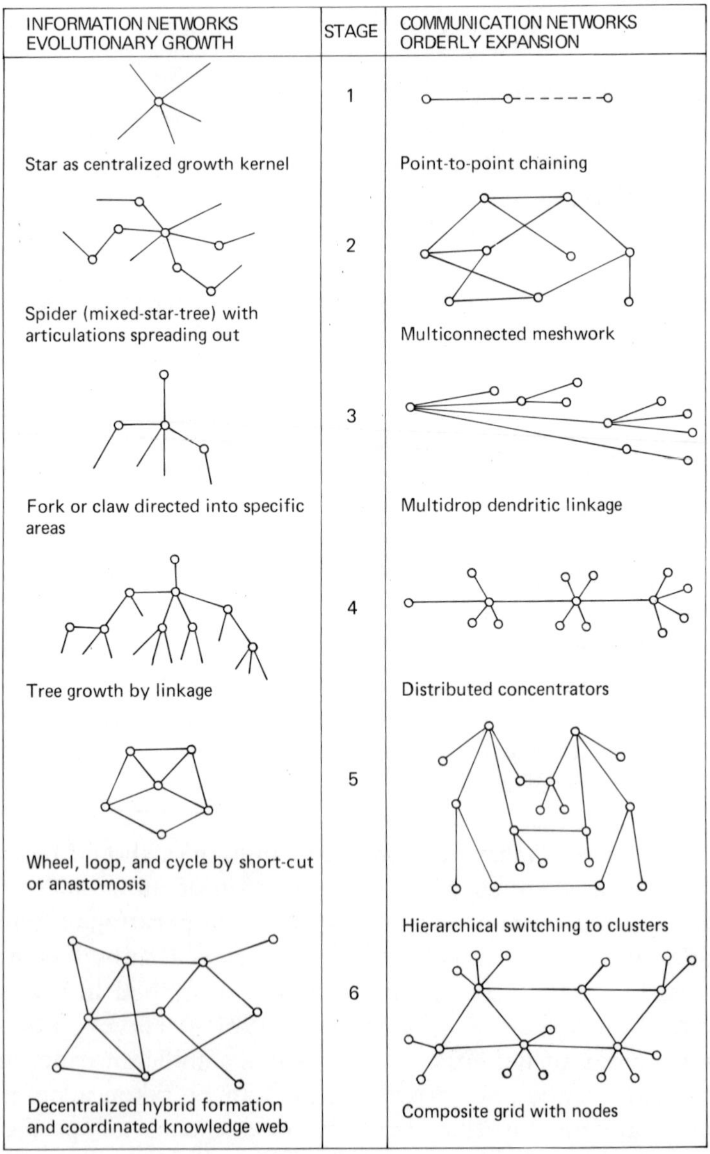

| INFORMATION NETWORKS EVOLUTIONARY GROWTH | STAGE | COMMUNICATION NETWORKS ORDERLY EXPANSION |
|---|---|---|
| Star as centralized growth kernel | 1 | Point-to-point chaining |
| Spider (mixed-star-tree) with articulations spreading out | 2 | Multiconnected meshwork |
| Fork or claw directed into specific areas | 3 | Multidrop dendritic linkage |
| Tree growth by linkage | 4 | Distributed concentrators |
| Wheel, loop, and cycle by short-cut or anastomosis | 5 | Hierarchical switching to clusters |
| Decentralized hybrid formation and coordinated knowledge web | 6 | Composite grid with nodes |

FIG. 6. Network morphology for information and communication.

isms for networks. Nevertheless, there exist many factors, parameters and variables that have a bearing on the quantity and quality of network properties. Most crucial are, as always, the seven M's i.e. Men, Machines, Materials, Money, Messages, Methods and Measurement. By these we mean:

| | |
|---|---|
| Men | —the key element forever in all systems remains personnel and manpower. |
| Machines | —including computers, and any other processing technology or facilities. |
| Materials | —including raw materials, supply, utilities and other energy forms. |
| Money | —financial resources in monetary terms are also represented as a kind of information. |
| Messages | —representing the various kinds of information and ideas. |
| Methods | —including procedures and documented know-how. |
| Measurement | —for test and evaluation when possible, but otherwise the assessment of observables. |

## 9.1. Information networks

As indicated above, the prime concern in international undertakings of informational joint-ventures is information networks. Paradoxically, they mainly exist as "schemes and dreams" more than as implemented operations (Samuelson, 1970). The reason is simple. Information exists all over the world in packaged form (books, documents, periodicals etc.) but cannot be rapidly transmitted or handled in a consorted way. The technological openings due to broadband telecommunications and digital computers are of so recent an age that they could not possibly have been implemented on a worldwide basis.

Today's information networks are usually built from nodes such as databases, library storage or large files, that are continuously updated, extended and maintained. Altogether the nodes function as a stack, divided into manageable, distributed portions that are organized and processed in a more efficient way (e.g. inverted files) than just a pile of knowledge. We recognize three basic elements (Fig. 7):

| | | |
|---|---|---|
| MB | Masterbases | The original, centralized stores of full information divided into major content fields. Retrieval time is quite long and "cold" storage costs are moderately low. |
| DB | Databases | The decentralized, retail stores that are tapped from masterbases, and mainly contain current information or surrogates. Retrieval time is swift and the more costly "hot" files are used for SDI. |
| RS | Relay-Switches | Specialized databases with locator files, may guide the information seeker to the most appropriate, likely and relevant database or masterbase. The very first entry may be facilitated through a manual, catalog-type referral-directory. |

It is worth noting that in contrast to telecommunication practices, the RS is not used for traffic or transit switching to a known address, but for directory look-up in locator files i.e. a specialized database that can tell where the address is, if it eventually exists; or be used for query-testing to indicate the likely trade-off of hits.

In practice, the inter-database organization for MB and DB tends to become hierarchical because of the supply diffusion from the masterbases to the distributed retail data-

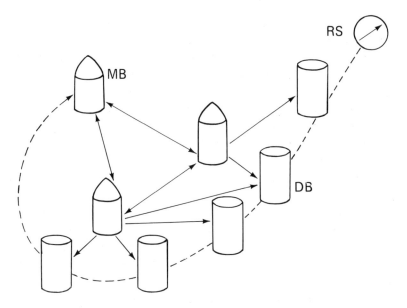

FIG. 7. Information network.

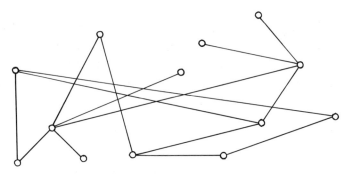

FIG. 8. Communication network.

bases. Often, the access-direction and search-routing run the opposite way, unless non-urgent but exhaustive and retrospective search is ordered primarily. The present situation for our information networks is that the processing of the DB's and MB's at the nodes is done through locally existing computers which are not interconnected and may in fact never be, for quite some time.

Developed information networks would cover any and all stored media (papers, records, films, audio, pictures, video, microforms etc.) in office desks, home drawers, institutions (libraries, archives, hospitals, TV-stations, record companies, publishing houses) in all countries. An "information utility" would consist of bidirectional free flow of information to and from the ultimate, everyday user i.e. any human being on this planet. By nature, the world's societal institutions are the first to gain from improved telecommunications. There is some risk that such interconnection between centralized storage units takes precedence over "the little man's" facilities, so that "big-sized inter-coms" are developed between institutions, ivory towers and established buildings. Thus another kind of network is equally important, namely the communication network.

### 9.2. Communication networks

Communication networks have existed for ages and centuries. The very early communication networks became a matter of point-to-point chaining, by the use of fires placed on top of dispersed mountains. Then came the use of smoke signals and multipoint distribution of sounds created by means of jungle drums.

There have existed a great variety of communication networks for many years (Fig. 8). The most wellknown ones are the widespread telecommunications represented by the common carriers, telephones, TELEX, TWX, TELPAK etc.

or mass communication, such as TV or CATV. Lately a number of radiolinks, intercoms and picturephones have come into existence. The service stations and outlet units are globally distributed among millions of organizations and people who have reasons for communicating. The communication networks in general do not have facilities for information storage, processing and computation like the other kinds of networks. Global communication networks are as distributed as can be.

Today we have grown so accustomed to the use of telephones, intercoms, walkie-talkies, radio and TV that we hardly think of the underlying network patterns of communication. The communication networks are characterized by the manifold of channel links. The information networks described in the past section (9.1) were dominated by the diversity of information kinds stored at a multitude of distributed nodes. In the past, the communication networks have had limited possibilities of storing or delaying the transmitted messages. This situation is changing due to the growing impact of a third kind of net, namely computer networks.

## 9.3. Computer networks

The early stages of shared computer facilities have generally been a matter of multiple-access, time-share centers (Figs. 9 and 10). These have originally had a starshape from which they have proliferated through tree-growth into spider-like configurations. Such configurations have often been ill-termed as "networks". In more worthwhile efforts, several "stars" of time-share computers have been linked at geographical distance. This is the beginning of true computer networks. The main advantage has been the possibility of sharing and giving additional core storage or occasionally software and application programs. A major advantage is the extra fall-back possibilities and increased reliability. There has been a widespread misuse of the concept "computer

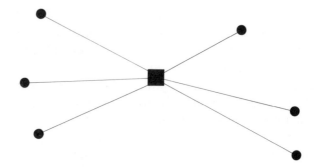

FIG. 9. Star as centralized growth kernel.

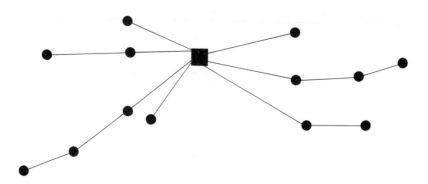

FIG. 10. Spider (mixed-star-tree) spreading its tentacles.

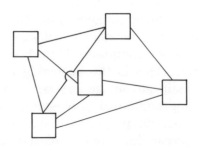

FIG. 11. Computer network.

utility". Newspaper stories have tried to give an impression that computer terminals for home use would make the average housewife a happy programmer, calculating "optimal" compositions of food ingredients before placing an on-line order for grocery delivery. The average human being is not likely to make calculated everyday moves, but would rather continue to make judgements based on ethics, taste and intuition.

Then, what is the nature of existing programs and data at the existing timeshare centers? Here is a typical list:

Simulation packages and data,
Optimization techniques and subroutines,
Homemade programming languages (ill-documented),
Chess-playing programs,
War-game subroutines,
Number-crunching programs,
Question–answering via subset languages for small limited fields,
Artificial Intelligence programs,
Theorem proving packages,
Pay-roll data,
Tax collector's data.

The kind of information that the average user wants is stored by some of the above information networks (Section 9.1). The nature of information is:

(a) Home and community information,
(b) Educational material,
(c) News and entertainment,
(d) Encyclopedia and handbook-type material,
(e) Professional guidelines and data,
(f) Scientific, technical, economic and research-oriented material,
(g) Tourist information,
(h) Audio-pictographic output etc.

There will be many years before a sufficient amount of all the above listed categories can be made available through computer set-ups. Meanwhile there will be new and different computer generations shifting perhaps as frequently as ever before i.e. every third year. These coming years will provide a valuable playground for experiments with software convertibility, hardware compatibility, terminal interface, store-and-forward, message-switching etc. Such large-scale experimenting is valuable for long-range improvements of serviceability, convenience, reliability and above all for the "hands-on" training of programmers and maintenance technicians.

There exist a number of time-shared computers, that have been interlinked into networks (Fig. 11). Such computer networks have dozens of local user terminals connected to each node computer. The size of the user population that can be reached is limited. The prime reasons for computer networking have been, increased reliability or fallback and shared software or CPU utilization. Sofar, only to a smaller extent has the interconnection contributed to the sharing of information, data and files between users at remotely distant computer nodes. The computer networks are gradually improving with respect to packet-switching, "intelligent terminals" and interface message processing. Also, new technologies, microprocessors and minicomputer generations are appearing that lead to structural changes. Hitherto some computer networks existed that do not have retrieval packages and that contain no information or data of the kind handled by the information networks. These circumstances do well justify that a distinction is made.

A solemn warning should be raised against excessive money spending on giant computers and ground communications. The same warning should be spelled out against investing in paper documents, libraries and buildings. Instead, the recommendable financing should go into worldwide, broadband telecommunications on a multipoint person-to-person basis, rather than traditional telephone traffic.

Another kind of computer application which is but one-directional though sometimes net-shaped can be found in terms of mass-media i.e. news publishers and TV. It is acceptable that little effort is spent on retrieval and storage of short-lived messages. More concern should, however, be given to possibilities of closing the loop i.e. allowing the receiver to talk back, possibly via computer terminals and telephones.

There is little excuse for those profit-making printers of scientific journals, catalogs and surrogates, who use computers as "the world's fastest typewriter" for open-loop distribution. Serious scientific publishers ought to know better and should guarantee retrieval possibilities from their output products instead of adding to the paper deluge with no concern about worldwide housekeeping, purging and recycling.

## 9.4. Relational networks

The past three networks for information, communications and computers respectively represent physical networks. The ultimate use of information is better thought of as for the support of relational networks. These are of logical rather than physical nature and represent the relations between individuals, divisions, departments, offices, organizations, areas, regions, nations etc. (Chapters 7 and 8). The relational networks often serve as a frame of reference, that the systems analyst can use during the design phase of his work. The logical structure then becomes a target scheme, the mapping of which is later implemented as a physical network, depending on the level of ambition for the final design. For every network the ultimate solution tends to be a compromise between desirability as derived from the logical relational network and feasibility as realized through the physical information and communication networks. The best known example of a relational network is the citation index (see Section 7.4.2). For retrieval purposes its main drawback is the inherent bias and the incompleteness due to gaps that eliminate actually existing relations.

There exist an exponential number of relations between people and activities in this world. Although most of the relations cannot be formalized there are some that lend themselves to description in terms of relational networks. The familiar types are routes, schemes, sociograms, ethnical bonds, organization charts, at the macro-level and logical files, associative linkages, cognitive maps, thesaurus structures, classificatory ordering schedules etc. at the micro-level. We shall mainly consider the macro-level logical networks.

### 9.5. Network hybrids

The existing networks can reasonably well be distinguished by their nature and properties as described above. Tomorrow's international networks will be hybrids i.e. an ambiguous blend of all those categories. Hopefully we shall see some examples of bidirectional, mixed multimedia networks characterized by the following elements and features:

(a) Coexistence of subsystems, regardless of their sophistication;

(b) Conviviality despite a certain lack of cooperation/coordination;

(c) Partial automation, depending on the application;

(d) Partial handling by professional mediators, depending on application and developmental stage;

(e) Closing of the loop between some endogenous and some exogenous information;

(f) Manageable network complexity;

(g) Sufficient availability/accessibility of information;

(h) Variety of media, channels and carriers;

(i) Tolerable density and aggregation of information items and output;
(j) Relay-switch databases and manual referral directories;
(k) Multilingual conversion tools.

Most of the above issues are selfdescriptive but nevertheless a few of them deserve special comments. The nature of "internationalism" in networks is such that people will have to live side-by-side despite some discrepancies and lack of understanding. Certain cultural socio-economic, geo-political and ethnic barriers will always exist. In fact, such barriers can sometimes be higher between institutions and groups in a particular country and less prevalent between nations. It is well known that there may exist intolerance, pride, esteem and personal envy between professions and trades as diverse as engineers, scientists, chemists, physicians, psychiatrists, psychologists, social workers, businessmen, ministers, priests etc. in other words, people who "ought to know better". Nationally they might experience a competitive environment, whereas internationally they would receive recognition. Opposed group representatives might sometimes become more open, when brought together by "neutral" intermediary elements at the interface with an information system.

### 9.5.1. Complexity

The concept of network complexity has several practical aspects to it. Complexity generally depends on the number of interconnections. A high amount of links often indicates a high degree of complexity. Sometimes the relative complexity is a better expression i.e. the number of interconnections compared to the number of nodes. From a maintenance point of view it is of course difficult to track down and repair a specific link among a number of multidirectional interconnections. Just think for instance about all the trouble one may have to go through for checking and to eventually reset some elements in isolated regions being part of an international network. Complexity can on the other hand be used to safeguard the system. A higher degree of complexity and redundant nodes or elements would contribute to an increased overall reliability and safety.

## 9.5.2. Ordering systems

Even a moderate degree of complexity calls for the use of ordering devices. The term "ordering" or "ordering systems" is adopted from Toman (1970) to stand for any method or tools for the purpose of "introducing order before placing an order for information", thus covering, e.g. classifications, thesauri, charts, catalogs, directories, entry-lists, look-up tables etc. When the user has a high number of alternate routes to chose from, he may want to address a relay-switch (Samuelson, 1971a), that can be a specialized database referring him to the sources or databases that are somewhat likely to hold his requested information. He may also need a handy, pocketsize referral-directory as a manual and crude first-entry device. Quite obviously international information and communication networks are faced with a linguistic problem. If this problem was to be handled to perfection it could indeed become cumbersome and costly. Since machine translation is not yet economically feasible other solutions have been suggested. One proposal is the development of multilingual thesauri and classifications. They could well be coupled to the above mentioned referral and switching methods. When a network is based on a single technology, say digital computers and textual data transmission, these external referral and switching devices can create an extensive problem. If, however, mixed multimedia networks are created there are always additional openings, that make it possible to bypass some bottlenecks. The fastest and least expensive way of communication is achieved when one does not necessarily try to squeeze bulky texts through digital computers.

### 9.5.3. Network density

In order to provide for sufficient availability and accessibility of information the number of service outlets generally must be increased which in turn may lead to higher complexity of the network. A higher degree or complexity can often be accepted if distance between the nodes is long enough, so that "cluttering" or aggregation can be avoided. This property of information networks is sometimes expressed as complexidense or some other measure of density (Samuelson, 1969, 1973).

The world's many countries, will reach different levels of network sophistication. In order to communicate internationally certain temporary arrangements for "ad hoc" interconnection should be allowed i.e. efforts in closing the loops between linked databases, online libraries, radio, TV, CATV and other media.

CHAPTER 10

# Netting and Development

The road toward operational networks is by and large a chain of procedural steps. Each of these steps is heavily dependent on an outlined methodology for guidance in system analysis terms. One can distinguish a developmental phase of netting, that actually is a blend of design, judgement, negotiations, compromise, artwork, "knitting" and predictive assessment at the office desk. The methodological procedures are basically the ones described in detail in the introductory chapters of this book. Some of the issues that have to be weighed deal with the mixture of centralization versus decentralization before arriving at an appropriate balance of the construct. Once the netting and development has been pursued one arrives at a successor phase of net-working. The net-working means just that, namely putting the net to work or making it work for its users toward fulfilment of defined objectives and operational goals.

## 10.1. Decentralization

The main reasons for entering joint information development programs and international netting have been indicated in the previous sections. One major reason for netting is the

89

idea of decentralized control and independence of functions that are nevertheless interrelated. Systems and subsystems that form part of a network may be controlled or uncontrolled, whereas the overall network at least has some points with loose control and perhaps a few junctions that occasionally require a more strict control. As a rule, the major obstacles against "free flow of information" is overemphasis of protocol, auditing, formalities, censorship and quality control. If such rules of procedure are considered necessary they should be managed at the local, national subsystems level, but preferably not at the international level.

## 10.2. Netting from scratch

In agreement with the above outlined systems design principles one can either start netting and development from scratch or build on some existing subsystem and operations. It is tempting to jump to the conclusion that money would be saved by developing networks from a few centralized growth kernels such as traditional libraries, data centers, computers and communication technology. This could become a disastrous mistake. There is always a tendency of using additional financial resources to cover some existing "hole" or bureaucracy rather than for the true purpose of research and development. There often exists an interest by established institutions to allow as long a period as possible for the depreciation of earlier investments. These two circumstances plus the fact that peers, executives and financial decision-makers are not aware of the latest technological growth potentials can stop worthwhile network schemes. The foundations of this statement is quite human and has been expressed and formulated by C.E.K. Mees, an Englishman, who was for many years vice-president for research at Kodak, who said:

> The best person to decide what research work shall be done is the man who is doing the research, and the next best person is the head of the

department who knows all about the subject and the work; after that, you leave the field of the best people and start on increasingly worse groups, the first being the research director who is probably wrong more than half the time, and then a committee which is wrong most of the time; and finally a committee of vice-presidents of the company itself which is wrong all the time. (Hall, 1969)

Designing and developing the networks from scratch can at first sight seem costly, especially when financial backing might not be easily raised in the beginning. On the other hand, latest technology will account for a longer systems lifecycle. Moreover, the development costs may become lower due to the additive benefits achieved from and intrinsic to the netting idea itself. The design and development of networks from scratch is also the best way of avoiding some other traditional traps and vicious circles.

## 10.3. Netting from kernels

Although the basic idea of netting is decentralization one sometimes is forced to build a network from a few growth kernels like "stars", "spiders" or "trees" (Figs. 6, 9, 10 and 12). Sometimes the avoidance of overlap is quoted as a reason for such tendencies. Certain distinctions should be made though. Overlap of input efforts should be minimized and avoided unless comparative quality control and evaluation is of prime concern. Overlap avoidance would justify the creation of decentralized input to networks such as INIS and ERIC. When it comes to output operations a truly international workload can only be sufficiently met by major network nodes in an amount ranging from three and up, depending on the economical conditions. An existing institution should not be allowed to take on additional information processing, storage and surrogates unless it is prepared to offer improved retrieval, extended opening hours and serviceability as well.

## 10.4. Balanced netting

The balanced growth, expansion and evolution of networks is handled according to different principles for the three networks types i.e. information, communication and computer nets. Information nets with stored information and databases are principally node-dominated. This means that their relative complexity is high i.e. each node has many links. The communication networks are generally link-dominated meaning that their relative complexity is lower and the number of links in proportion to nodes is not that high. The computer networks will continue to go through various stages of metamorphosis since they are constantly subject to change, for optimization reasons. As computer generations come and disappear, their networks are orderly superimposed upon the irregular web of information networks that has deep roots among people, services, disciplines and community functions in all countries.

## 10.5. Satisficing

Computer networks will remain subject to time/cost minimization and traffic optimization. The network hybrids of information and multimedia communication networks due to their human-oriented and people-dependent nature will have to be approached through methods of satisficing throughout their development. The principle of satisficing deserves some further explanation (Simon, 1970, Langefors, 1973). The essence of satisficing is a matter of settling for fair or better instead of for best. It is a practical way of dealing with actual design situations for information networks. This will effect not only the efficiency with which resources for designing are used, but also the nature of the final network design as well. Each nation's satisficing value—the degree of fulfillment of a given information need that will permit the nation to go on to devote conscious attention to the next higher-order need—is different for various need levels. This circumstance again ties into the earlier reasoning about higher objectives now in terms of individual as well as national goals.

CHAPTER 11

# Networking and Perspectives

The true challenge occurs when it comes to making the net really work. Work toward the implementation of a few international networks as described above, has so far been met with enthusiasm due to the worthwhile nature of such schemes. A few fragmentary networks for computers, data transmission and information input or partial, limited output have come into existence (Samuelson, 1975a). The fullfledged network hybrids with widespread operational information output as a utility still remain the tasks of this decade. We have already made a clear distinction between computer center availability and a veritable information utility. The road towards an international information utility goes gradually through the following protracted stages:

(1) Network planning,
(2) Network design, and implementation,
(3) Marketing and service promotion,
(4) Education and training,
(5) Information utility.

Each step from (1) to (4) is a compulsory precedent before the ultimate stage (5) can be reached. It is therefore easy to understand that utility from international networks is a many troubled scheme.

## 11.1. Network planning

When the systems analyst is engaged in the planning of a network he must seek for it, that a documented methodology over the procedural steps is made available and covers all the succedent net-working stages that can be anticipated. There will always be surprise events, but by and large the network planning should follow the methodology given in Chapter 3. Although a majority of the physical implementation, equipment selection and materials acquisition is not handled until after the final design stage, there are a few basic issues of the "materialized end product" that will have to be conceived earlier. The practical and physical nature is operationally visualized, so to speak. This creation or construct has sometimes not been thoroughly questioned before the project is started. Often the initial concept is based on dated technology with too low a level of ambition. A few cases from the field of information are therefore reviewed in brief, mainly as a warning to any planning that is not farsighted enough. The examples are chosen in arbitrary order:

Extensive production and storage of microfiche have been undertaken for wellfounded reasons. However, a widespread availability of fichereading displays and hardcopy printout has not been sought for.

Zip code assignment has been requested in many countries but a wide enough distribution of code directories has not been guaranteed. Neither are inquiry desks or services easily available.

Online bibliographic retrieval installations are being promoted for quick delivery of surrogates. Little or no coupling has been made to those collections, that would guarantee a fair chance of delivering the full information when desirable.

Similarly, new library buildings or referral centers have been established without providing enough distributed service stations or extended service hours.

Academically educated indexers and search-formulators have been persuaded to work within the information field. They have not been given the appropriate motivation through career planning, job openings and promotion to advanced positions.

One might claim as an excuse the fact that the information field is quite new. However, the effects quoted above could have been foreseen, since in essence they are by no means exclusive to the field of information. Indeed, these adverse effects and mistakes are good reasons for emphasizing the necessity of "information science" as an applied science in a fully professional sense.

## 11.2. Network design

As indicated by the first few chapters of this book international network design is a typical job for information systems analysts. An international information network is probably one of the largest size projects a systems analyst could be faced with. The parameters, variables and concepts are numerous and will have to be taken into account when the design phase is started. At an early stage, and then iteratively the systems analyst will have to review similar or related designs and operations, in order to derive their pros and cons. To date there hardly exist any ultimate designs for information networks. A few typical, preliminary examples are lifted from teleprocessing, some having certain limitations to the growth potentials as shown in Figs. 9–16. The disadvantage of network growth from the structures in Figs. 9, 10, 12 and 14 are due to the early tendency of centralization. Yet, the spread of a star into a spider has been tried nationally. Symptomatic to this trend a few hierarchies have been tried, and the spiders sometimes grow tree-like tentacles, that like claws become directed into specific areas, regions, applica-

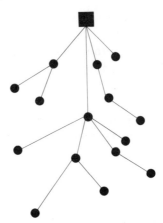

FIG. 12.  Tree hierarchy.

FIG. 13.  Distributed multidrop line.

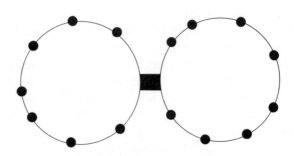

FIG. 14.  Loop transmission.

tions or subject fields. In the case of teleprocessing the centralization trends have been caused by the scarcity of giant computer financing and maintenance. The similar behavior might occur to information networks if they were to be grown from a few single libraries or established institutions. Figs. 15 and 16 show some later and anticipated trends for computer and communication networks.

If the net is centralized or the relative complexity is high, the more sensitive or vulnerable to node-damage is the network, which is a good reason against over-centralization. Damage or misuse of a centralized node would affect a major section of the overall network. In contrast, the effects on a decentralized design, becomes less hazardous. We hasten to say that this general design principle refers to an international information utility from networks. For limited and internal corporate use a certain degree of centralization can sometimes be well justified. Alternative options are advantageous for the larger national and international user situations. Here, in order to avoid a star-spider spread, the new and potential users might actually be advised to join two or three different and partially competitive networks.

## 11.3. Network marketing and promotion

Network ideas for information, computers and communications are mainly untried and non-tested in a multitude of nations. It is reasonable that there exists towards networks a certain scepticism and some inertia locally as well as regionally. Consequently, the effort needed for marketing and promotion may be considerable. This is much due to the fact that the final product and service is seldom available for demonstration. Moreover, the potential user will have to be persuaded that the temporary product is useful. Perhaps the main obstacle is the eternal fact, that the usefulness of information is so difficult to prove. It is not realized until the

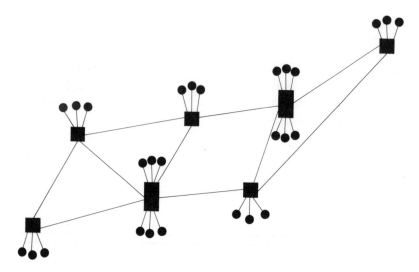

FIG. 15.  Decentralized grid.

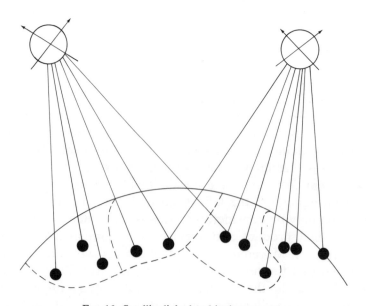

FIG. 16.  Satellite-linked multipoint networks.

service is temporarily withdrawn or no longer available.

In terms of marketing and promotion there is sometimes just one practical way to follow, namely make a temporary installation for trial use. This can sometimes be arranged for communications and computers. When it comes to full information the test service often becomes too extensive. Each installation has a certain personnel requirement and this tends to be even more extensive when it comes to information systems and networks built from such systems and subsystems. Altogether the marketing and promotion may amount to the same order as planning and design.

## 11.4. Education and training

When it comes to education and training of personnel, who are intended for work on an information net, this is just as time consuming and sometimes equally costly as marketing and promotion (see Section 7.5.1). Internationally the timewise protraction is the dominant issue, due to the following reasons:

(a) Course material has to be prepared.

(b) Teachers and expert instructors must be hired, sponsored and sometimes given a "brush up".

(c) A language barrier may exist, that affects educational material, teachers' communication and applicability of the information product itself.

(d) Appropriately sized and composed groups of trainees must be brought together at a feasible time and place.

(e) The time gap between early training and operationally implemented results is considerable.

Despite the above listed difficulties there exist a few bright hopes. At least some introductory educational material in the six or seven major languages could be packaged and integrated as a modular part of the information systems themselves. This approach would hardly be cost-effective for the more specialized jobs and skills that are performed by a small group of people. Neither would it be applicable to material that requires updating, unfortunately an often existing case.

If, however, the very first lecture is outlined as an "everybody's introduction" the instructional material represents a methodology link between promotion and education, serving both purposes.

Continuous education is perhaps best performed through synoptic, brush-up courses in the field of Information Management. Such courses can be derived from the various course modules already existing in postgraduate, interdisciplinary Masters programs and University curricula in Information Science or Informatics. As an example of a core curriculum geared at a Masters of SCI (Systems, Cybernetics and Informatics) the following from Stockholm University and Royal Institute of Technology is significant (Samuelson, 1971c, 1975c):

(1) General Systems, Cybernetics and Informatics,
(2) Information Systems Analysis and Design,
(3) Information Management and Retrieval,
(4) Industrial Information and Organizational Control,
(5) Information Networks and Teleprocessing,
(6) Interactive Human-Computer Communications,
(7) Data Security and Integrity in Systems,
(8) International Information Transfer and Telesatellites,
(9) Thesis and Design Implementation.

*Definition.* INFORMATICS stands for Information Science and Technology, defined as that field which includes: Structure and properties of information and communication as well as theory and methods for the transfer, organizing, storage, retrieval, evaluation and distribution of information, and furthermore information systems, nets, processes and

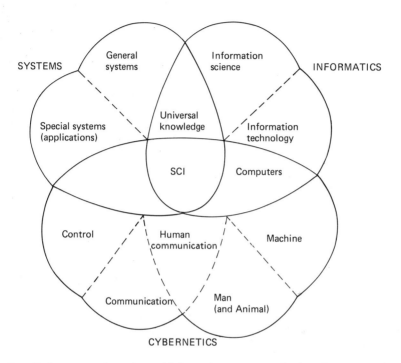

FIG. 17. Systems, cybernetics and informatics as an emerging breed, to master the information systems dynamics occurring at the fields intersection.

activities that mediate knowledge from source to user and are based on general systems, cybernetics, automation, and technology for human work environments in timely and current praxis.

Typical course modules and topics derived from the major fields (Fig. 17) are:

Information Systems,
Communication Systems,
Human Communication,
Human Information Processing,
Living Systems,
Social Systems,

Man–machine Systems,
Man–machine Communication,
Control Systems,
Computing Machines,
Computer Systems,
Computer Communication,
Library Systems,
Management Systems,
Management Information Systems,
Organizational Control Systems,
Information Management,
Vocabulary Control Systems (Thesauri),
Special Classification Systems,
Universal Classification Systems,
Global Knowledge Systems,
etc.

The gist of such a trans-scientific and meta-level curriculum is that it can be understood by a multitude of postgraduate students having previous academic degrees from fields as diversified as: Business administration, electrical engineering, library service, law school, industrial psychology, medicine, biosciences, etc.

The bibliographic references of our book cover journal articles, monographs and select chapters on information systems and networks. There exist but a few text books that somewhat sufficiently cover the gist of General Systems, Cybernetics, Information Networks and Management, such as:

| General Systems | (Society for General Systems Research, Yearbook, 1956–1975) (van Gigch, 1974) (Miller, 1976) |
| --- | --- |

| | |
|---|---|
| Cybernetics | (Schoderbek and Kefalas, 1975) |
| | (Beer, 1975) |
| Organization and Management | (Cleland and King, 1972) |
| | (Kast and Rosenzweig, 1970) |
| Management Information Systems | (Murdick and Ross, 1975) |
| | (Davis, 1974) |
| | (Matthews, 1976) |
| Information Systems Analysis | (Alexander, 1974) |
| | (Horton, 1974) |
| | (Fitzgerald and Fitzgerald, 1973) |
| | (Langefors and Samuelson, 1976). |

## 11.5. Information utility

In previous sections we have made a clear distinction between computer utilization and the usefulness of information. When the highly ambitious concept "information utility" is coming within reach it will have a somewhat different meaning nationally and internationally. There is always a service side to information activities and the real utility of information will to a certain extent depend on the local and regional conditions. Moreover, there are a manifold of specific information kinds, and due to their strictly national dependence and domestic ties it would not be feasible to make them available internationally. Although situations sometimes occur when global availability/accessibility may be desirable, there generally exist trade-off points that in a natural way dictate the priorities for implementation. Today only some of the potentially useful information exists in libraries, which indicates that tomorrow's information centers, data-bases and libraries will have to adjust to the overall demands on a so called information utility. For a comparison we shall first review in a listed presentation those information activities that are of obvious international concern. A second list shows the nature of that information which has national, geopolitical or sociocultural bonds.

In an arbitrary order the following fields could form the basis of an international information utility:

Airline information,
Weather data,
Environmental quality information,
Trade center service,
Tourist information,
Hotel reservations,
Medical and health-care information to support practising physicians in telemedicine,
International publishing and massmedia (TV, newspapers, CATV),
Stockbrokerage news,
Banking and financial information,
Police information (Interpol),
Insurance information.

The following information activities are less likely contributions to internationalism due to the overruling domestic bonds:

Railroad, bus and other local, public transportation details,
Employment information and job matching,
Most data contained in hospital information systems (HIS),
Social workers' data,
Local mass media and brochure or folder distribution,
Provincial library and archive material,
Nation-specific law texts,

Defence and intelligence information,
Religious, monolingual material.

A comparison of those two lists over issues and information activities shows some obvious indications for information centers, new library-like operations, data bases or whatever they might be called. Serviceability and convenience and mode of output for the information have a high ranking. Surrogates, indexes and directories will continue to be advantageous but only if they are used for referral purposes as a means of closing the loop and furthering the communication of full information. The individual handling and management of the information systems prove to be increasingly important. A valuable and well designed system, originated in one country can get a bad reputation through poor management and nursing in another nation. The eventual success is often left completely in the hands of some host administration or institution. Yet, this is better than any attempts to create supranational bodies. Let us review the above list of desirable issues that have *development potentials*. Certain priorities can be formulated on the basis of universal interests. The nonprofit information products and services lend themselves best for international undertakings in cooperation and eventually also coordination in a few cases.

With regard to the information contents there were initially outspoken priorities given to scientific and technological information (STI). Later, economic documents were included and the key issue became scientific, technological and economic information (STEI). A quick glance at the above lists for information utility shows that STI is only a fraction. It may turn out costly not to be able to include information of societal and community interest, at some later date. Even if the original design target would just be STI, the systems analyst should have an idea of future growth possibilities, the present system lifecycle and extendability into coverage of socio-economic, behavioral and life sciences.

Although it is somewhat difficult to categorize the various prototype information systems such crude class distinctions are sometimes used, and they are:

(a) Discipline-oriented information systems
(b) Mission-oriented information systems
(c) Dedicated information systems
(d) Action-oriented information systems

A short discription of the meaning of those concepts may be appropriate.

### 11.5.1 Discipline-oriented information systems

The discipline-oriented information systems have their roots in academic disciplines. Originally they could be clearly separated in fields such as physics, economics, humanities etc. The discipline-oriented information activities have often been input-oriented, and input for information storage is frequently handled by arrangements of certain societies, associations or federations. As new interdisciplinary and multidisciplinary fields develop the original separations tend to lose their meanings.

### 11.5.2. Mission-oriented information systems

The mission-oriented information systems originally arose by demand from professional groups where the members discovered that they jointly had a need for certain kinds of information. It did not particularly matter where the information came from as long as it was relevant. This kind of information actually has been mainly output-oriented. There has been a tendency of those information stores to become amorphous so that the original idea to some extent has been lost. In more specific terms one might say that relevance has decreased in proportion to recall from information retrieval and dissemination.

## 11.5.3. Dedicated information systems

Sometimes the term dedicated has been used for information systems and networks. The meaning of the word has, however, been used differently depending on the "dedication". Some authors have said that e.g. an information system for Environmental Quality is dedicated, since it is specific and yet would cut right across many disciplines and missions. Other sources use the word "dedicated" for equipment and technology e.g. telex, radio, CATV. Thus, some of the various techniques for communication networks are sometimes described as "dedicated", meaning that they can only handle certain kinds of information and messages due to their physical properties and design constraints. For instance, a telesatellite for bidirectional multipoint, person-to-person live communication and retrieval of audio-pictographic material would be termed dedicated (Samuelson, 1971b).

## 11.5.4. Action-oriented information systems

In terms of a network based information utility the most adequate design would come from multiple action-oriented information systems. Action-oriented has a pragmatic meaning and is applicable to most activities specified above in the two lists of section 11.5. Information stored in an action-oriented system generally releases some observable physical action at the time for the message delivery (Samuelson, 1968). An international information utility would be created from many designs of action-oriented systems and subsystems, that all contribute to an international information network. Such a network should have as few mediators as possible in order not to delay action-taking by the ultimate user who is also the true decision-maker in charge of handling a specific situation. This approach gives priority to special-purpose applications although the design can be generalized. Also, the pragmatic side of information is emphasized more than the semantic and syntactic aspects. The international usefulness increases if the information is of such a nature that the action triggered by it is similar, regardless where in the world the decision situation exists. An action can be a service or a technology pursuance, or remote therapy prescription in telemedicine.

A similar approach to the use of information is declared by C. West Churchman who writes:

> In much of the popular literature about research and science, the authors often assume that the meaning of a "systematic collection of known facts" or "collection of information" is a clear concept to most readers. Apparently they think of a "collection" in terms of a library, and a systematic collection to be like a well-run library with an adequate indexing and cataloguing system. However, no library qualifies as an entity having a "state of knowledge" in the sense discussed above. It is true that stored in it are strings of meaningful symbols. But it has no adequate way of showing which strings are meaningful and which are true. We would have to say that the state of knowledge resides in the combined system consisting of the library and an astute and adept human user.

He continues:

> A library so designed that the retrieval of information is either impossible or much too time-consuming is *not* a collection of information, no matter how many correct sentences are stored there. It is not a collection, because it fails to provide the correct response, given a query. (Churchman, 1971)

CHAPTER 12

# *International Scope of Networks*

The real advantage and veritable benefit of networks is probably particularly achievable at the international level through network hybrids. The majority of national planners are, however, unaware of the potentials. When it comes to the blend of superimposed *information networks* of stored knowledge, *computer nets, telecommunications, relational nets* and human intellects we arrive at complex *network hybrids*. These hybrids are "constitutive" i.e. their characteristics are not "summative" but amount to much higher magnitudes than the sum of the isolated parts. The effect of adding information like STI to big-sized intercoms such as computer-computer nets is overwhelming. This plus the introduction of global telecommunication satellites for worldwide distributed networks means that through combinatory thinking we can advance to hitherto unforeseen levels of abstraction and new extensions of reasoning or augmenting of the intellect. Without STI this will never happen, as computers and telecommunications alone are not enough. STI and information science is the essential "bite" and catalyzer that must be integrated with the technological artifacts and the human mentefacts. With STI included there will be a symbiotic cross-fertilization and a reinforcement or amplification of each of the different network constituents. This leads to a complete revolution in scientific work methods with openings of new R & D approaches as global think tanks toward the fulfilment of human objectives and societal goals.

In order to get an idea of the approximate magnitude and constituents that make the global or worldwide network hybrids of information, telecommunication satellites, computers and intellects, some facts and size figures may be quoted (Samuelson, 1973) as reproduced in Fig. 18. The elements

| Nodal function | Element | Approximate magnitude |
|---|---|---|
| Relay-satellite |  | $h.10$ |
| Referral-switch, ground locator |  | $i.10^2$ |
| Masterbase |  | $j.10^3$ |
| Database |  | $k.10^4$ |
| Computer | | $1.10^5$ |
| Manual entry directory |  | $m.10^7$ |
| Users at service stations/terminals |  | $n.10^8$ |

FIG. 18. Global network elements.

displayed in Fig. 18 are the ones described in previous Chapters 9–11.

Faced with such a magnitude of elements, subsystems, functions, parameters and variables the systems analyst will have to pay even more attention to using formalized concepts during all phases of design, development and evaluation. He will have to be constantly aware of the evolution, complexity, flexibility, reliability, structural density etc. that relates to the intermeshed regional networks of different kinds. The nature of these system design concepts is reproduced in Fig. 19 (Samuelson, 1973), which indicates the differences between the network kinds defined in Chapters 9 and 10. By following the guidelines and formalized concepts the systems analyst will also get a feeling of building on a solid ground when designing such megasystems as global and worldwide networks.

The key element in information networks will always be

| Design feature | Information Networks | Computer Networks | Communica-Networks | Relational Networks |
|---|---|---|---|---|
| Evolution trend | Node dominated | Node dominated | Link dominated | Link dominated |
| Characteristic property | Few centralized nodes | Few distributed nodes | Many links | Many relations |
| Complexity | Low | Low | High | High |
| Relative complexity | High | Low | Low | High |
| Flexibility | Low | High | Low | Moderate |
| Node degree | Varying | Stable | Stable | Varying |
| Reliability | Low | High | High | Low |
| Accessibility | Low | High | High | Low |
| Structure | Hierarchical sometimes | Distributed | Distributed | Hierarchical sometimes |
| Density | Low | High | Low | High |
| Dependability | High | Low | Low | High |
| Efficiency | Low | High | High | Low |
| Use | Occasional | Occasional | Frequent | Frequent |
| Elements | Unique | Redundant | Redundant | Unique |

Fig. 19.

man himself. Networks are the typical case of general systems and applied cybernetics i.e. communication and control for the human use of human beings. Nevertheless there exist numerous cases were the opposite may happen through constellations of proliferating star-nets. Any network is doomed to fail, yield animosity and aggravations if it does not include already from the beginning everybody who has an interest in the design, development and pluralistic utilization. This has been studied in depth by Nielsen (1974a, 1974b) and collaborators. Particularly Nielsen and his researchers have observed the misbehavior of empire-builders, peers, operators, maneuverers and the likes, who "take the ball and run" in order to enlarge their domains, claims and vested interests. "Their motivation for starting another network focused on using it to support a larger and more powerful central facility for themselves." "No sooner is a small center established than a variety of efforts arise to expand it and shut off competition. The empire-builder's ambition do not stop there, for networking has broadened his horizons. Thus, he wants his computer itself to become the central facility for the network. Serving other users is also a means of obtaining additional revenue to support a larger in-house operation." In other words, an explicit advice to: "Beware of the empire-builders and juntas" is given by Nielsen et al. They continue to focus on other important issues, which are listed as follows:

(1) Older, successful networks are usually marked by a change in the decision-making structure and the outright ownership.

(2) Some approaches lead to partial ownership by all those participating or they become included in boards of directors.

(3) Change in control is imperative by the remote users.

(4) The facility will face more constraints in that way.

(5) The existence of a network makes people converse about mutual interests and information interchange is facilitated.

(6) A number of benefits quite far-removed from sharing computing power can be realized.

(7) There is a sharp discrepancy between the views of the central facility and the remote users.

(8) Everyone expects his institution to be a central facility, not a remote node. In that way there would be only central facilities and no remote or using nodes.

(9) There is a difficulty of having a central facility that is responsive to the remote users' needs and there is a lack of understanding as to their real concerns and the depths thereof.

(10) Changes, particularly the beneficial ones, are not automatic.

(11) A "closed club" may develop that thwarts broader involvment.

(12) Terminals are not as motivating as local computers.

(13) All too often, the central facilities accentuate the discontent by their own behavior.

(14) Users do not like being placed at the mercy of another organization and unless they gain some measure of control they may get off the network.

(15) A network can foster interaction between users at different remote sites because of the central-versus-remote conflict.

The above listed findings have implications for planning and design. An information network is not just a computer or telecommunication net. It is aimed for sharing all resources namely file contents, software, hardware, management, ownership by everybody who would like to participate today or in the next few years. It would be worse than foolish to repeat past years' mistakes i.e. installing a few processing nodes or maxi-computers and then hoping that later there will come enough terminals and traffic. Several such networks have become failures with too little traffic, too few users and all too costly maintenance of the few "empire nodes". They just become "big-size intercoms" for the node owners, who try to fill the overhead capacity with different kinds of processing jobs, all but what was originally intended as retrieval of knowledge. In fact, it is a typical case of feeding the Matthew effect: "To him who hath shall be given" i.e. the rich get richer and the have-nots get poorer. The age of institutionalization and so called "centers of excellence" is passé and their vested interests must not be added to.

Todays LSI circuits and electronic microminiaturization have caused 30% cost reduction and 10 times capacity increases in a year. This opens up completely new ways of network architecture and design. Fully distributed networks with minis, micro-computers and so called "intelligent terminals" installed "by the dozen" can be placed in offices, universities and labs right in the hands of the ultimate users who do not have to depend on some "expanding star or spider". Instead, the bidirectional user communication is facilitated and encouraged. Numerous alternate line topologies are plausible depending on the number of sites and reliability constraints. When background jobs for telefacsimile and routing searches of local holdings justify packet switching it becomes feasible e.g. to have a ring or trunk of leased lines through as many sites as possible with one-node bypass loops for fallback working on a dial-up basis as in Fig. 20. This can also be combined with regional or global telesatellite beams to yield multi-connected or fully connected networks respectively as suggested in Fig. 21. Then packet broadcasting and direct-receiving/sending, portable, pocket-size, "walkie-talkie-lookies" bring us closer to accessing globally distributed knowledge within forthcoming years. This approach is partially desirable, and feasible as well, for developing countries, geographically dispersed areas or islands, isolated regions and rural communities who are not hampered by outdated, preexistent telecommunications and computer technology.

Large-scale, world-wide information retrieval is here to stay. The availability of veritable information networks is

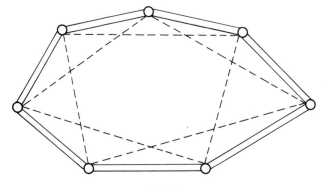

FIG. 20.

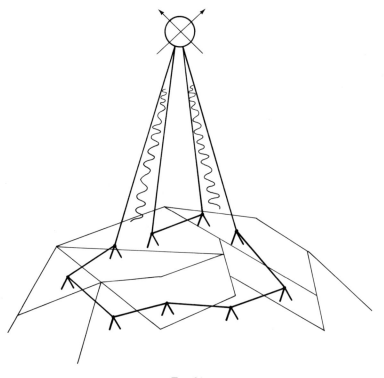

FIG. 21.

becoming a reality. The benefits are many, including resource-sharing and geographical independence. In fact, information itself is being recognized as a resource and an energy form. It is no longer just the processing facility and CPU-sharing that offers benefits. These are almost exceeded by the value of information stores gradually building up through international joint efforts.

There exist a number of computer nets and but a few information networks. They have all been described elsewhere, and the reader is referred to those writings, which are also cited among our bibliographic references. Wellknown projects of computer networks are GE-MARK III, AR-PANET, ALOHA, TYMNET, SITA, SWIFT, TELENET, INFONET, CYBERNET, CYCLADES, NPL and EIN (COST-11 project) as well as the information networks ESA-NET and LIBRIS or input-nets like INIS, AGRIS, ERIC, OCLC etc. Many of the networks are in a state of flux. Some are based on packet-switching or traditional line-switching while others are geared at data-base storage. We shall refrain from discussing their details since tomorrow's network structures and information systems architectures will look quite different based on telesatellites, digital packet-radio, portable walkie-talkie-lookies, intell-terminals ("intelligent" programmable terminals), microprocessors and clustered minicomputers to facilitate teleconferencing.

In summary, the international scope of information networks is extremely wide. Technology already exists here and now, but the road to network development is long and progress toward implementation is slow. The main obstacles are the conventional inhibits, red tape, protocol and bureaucratic administrative traditions. Other hindrances are due to vested interests in earlier techniques, materials and methods. Recent technology to some extent makes a few catalogs, indexes or surrogate packages superfluous. Nevertheless information systems are often designed without considering the on-going progress in communications. Some reasonably useful information retrieval systems have been designed. Even though it may superficially seem as if they were generally useful for multiple purposes, it turns out that they have quite severe limitations. There is a big risk that such systems become nationally controlled by various official bodies or governments who try to turn a temporary design into "Ein Mädchen für Alles". No information system is general enough. All existing systems designs have drawbacks either in terms of updating, maintenance, extendability, timeliness, versatility, flexibility, or convertibility. Standardization is beneficial only if it leaves enough free roads for further experiments, interconnectibility and multimedia interfaces, that may contribute to opening some existing gates and closing the feedback loops needed in international bidirectional communication as a way for free flow of information (UNESCO, 1969, Samuelson, 1974). To this end, worthwhile long-range programs like UNESCO's own UNISIST project have been launched (Atherton, 1976). Complementary thereto, perspective thinking has started toward WISE, i.e. a World Information Synthesis Encyclopedia (Kochen, 1975). When materialized, this idea can be thought of as nowadays extrapolation of Vannevar Bush's Memex or H. G. Wells' World Brain—indeed a commendable goal.

# References

Ackoff, R.L. (ed.), 1974. Systems and Management Annual 1974. Petrocelli/Charter, New York, 620 pp.

Adelson, M., 1968. The Systems Approach—A Perspective. Wilson Library Bulletin, March 1968, pp. 711–715. (For much of the discussion on the general characteristics of the systems approach, the author (Borko) is indebted to discussions with Marvin Adelson and his publications.)

Alexander, M.J., 1974. Information Systems Analysis, Theory and Applications. Science Research Associates, Palo Alto, Calif., 424 pp.

Amey, G.X., 1968. Channel Hierarchies for Matching Information Sources to Users' Needs. Proc. Annual Meeting of the American Society for Information Science in Columbus, Ohio, October 1968, pp. 11–14.

Amey, G.X., 1970. The Forgiving System—Human Aspects of System Planning. In: H. Borko et al., Systems Analysis, an Approach to Information, (Presented at FID Congress, Buenos Aires, 1970) Stockholm (FID No 480, TRITA-IBADB 5002).

Atherton, P., 1976. UNISIST Handbook. UNESCO, Paris.

Beach, T., 1967. How to Make a Systems Survey. The Office, September 1967.

Becker, H., 1973. Functional Analysis of Information Networks. Wiley, New York, 281 pp.

Beer, S., 1975. Platform for Change. Wiley, New York, 457 pp.

Beishon, J. and Peters, G. (eds.), 1972. Systems Behaviour. Open University Press, Harper and Row, New York, 320 pp.

Borko, H., 1972. The Nature of Networks. In: K. Samuelson et al., Global and Long-distance Decision-making, Environmental Issues and Network Potentials (FID/TM Panel at the ASIS 1971 Meeting in Denver), Stockholm (FID No 493, TRITA-IBADB 5003) pp. 11–27.

Borko, H., Schur, H., Amey, G. X. and Samuelson, K., 1970. Systems Analysis, an Approach to Information, (Presented at FID Congress, Buenos Aires, 1970) Stockholm (FID No 480, TRITA-IBADB 5002).

Carr, C.S., Crocker, S.D. and Cerf, V.G., 1970. HOST-HOST Communication Protocol in the ARPA Network. In: American Federation of Information Processing Societies Spring Joint Computer Conference, Atlantic City, N.J., May 1970, Proc., Vol. 36. Thompson, Washington, D.C., pp. 589–597.

Churchman, C.W., 1968. The Systems Approach. A Delta Book. Dell Publ., New York, 243 pp.

Churchman, C. W., 1971. The Design of Inquiring Systems, Basic Concepts of Systems and Organization. Basic Books, New York, 288 pp.

Churchman, C.W. and Wesner, R.W. (eds.), 1975. Systems and Management Annual 1975. Petrocelli/Charter, New York, 620 pp.

Cleland, D.I and King, W.R., 1972. Management, a Systems Approach. McGraw-Hill, New York, 442 pp.

Cleveland, H., 1972. The Future Executive. Harper and Row, New York.

Davis, G.B., 1974. Management Information Systems, Conceptual Foundations, Structure and Development. McGraw-Hill, New York, 482 pp.

Debons, A. (ed.), 1974. Information Science, Search for Identity. Marcel Dekker, New York, 491 pp.

Debons, A. and Cameron, W. (eds.), 1975. Perspectives in Information Science. NATO ASI Series No E10, Noordhoff, Groningen, 797 pp.

Dreyfus, H., 1972. What Computers Can't Do. Harper and Row, New York, 259 pp.

Engelbart, D.C., Watson, R.W. and Norton, J.C., 1973. The Augmented Knowledge Workshop. In: Proc. AFIPS Conf. New York 4–8 June 1973, AFIPS Press, Montvale, No. 7, pp. 9–21.

Fitzgerald, J.M. and Fitzgerald, A.F., 1973. Fundamentals of Systems Analysis. Wiley, New York, 531 pp.

Fried, L., 1972. Hostility in Organization Change. Journal of Systems Management, Vol. 23, No 6, pp. 14–21.

Garfield, E., 1964. Science Citation Index. Science, Vol. 144, No 3619, pp. 649–654.

General Systems Yearbook, 1956–1975. Vol. I-XX. SGSR, Society for General Systems Research. Washington, D.C.

Haggerty, P.E., 1969. Process of Technological Innovation. National Academy of Sciences, Washington, D.C.

Hall, P.D., 1969. Computer Systems. In: G. Wills et al. (eds.), Technological Forecasting and Corporate Strategy, Chapter 12, Bradford University Press, London, p. 192.

Hancon, J., 1971. Who Derailed the Duper-tube. New Scientist, pp. 151–153.

Horton, F.W., 1974. How to Harness Information Resources, a Systems Approach. Association for Systems Management, Cleveland, Ohio, 147 pp.

Jacobs, R.A., 1972. Putting "Manage" into Project Management. Journal of Systems Management, Vol. 23, No 1, pp. 20–25.

Kast, F.E. and Rosenzweig, J.E., 1970. Organization and Management, a Systems Approach. McGraw-Hill, New York, 654 pp.

King, D.W. and Bryant, E.C., 1971. The Evaluation of Information Services and Products. Information Resources Press, Washington, D.C., 306 pp.

Kochen, M. (ed.), 1975. Information for Action, from Knowledge to Wisdom. Academic Press, New York, 248 pp.

Langefors, B., 1973. Theoretical Analysis of Information Systems. Auerbach, Philadelphia, Pa., 489 pp.

Langefors, B. and Samuelson, K., 1976. Information and Data in Systems. Petrocelli/Charter, New York.

Matthews, D.Q., 1976. The Design of the Management Information System. Petrocelli/Charter, New York, 221 pp.

McCarn, D.B., 1970. Preparing the Organization for Automation. In: Problems of Mechanization of Small Information Centers, AGARD Conference Proc. No 57, pp. 35–42.

Melcher, A.J. (ed.), 1975, General Systems and Organization Theory, Methodological Aspects. Kent State·University Press, 123 pp.

Miller, J.G., 1971. The Nature of Living Systems. Behavioral Science, Vol. 16, pp. 277–301.

Miller, J.G., 1976. Living Systems. McGraw-Hill, New York.

Murdick, R.G. and Ross, J.E., 1975. Information Systems for Modern Management, 2nd ed. Wiley, New York, 671 pp.

Myers, J.S., 1971. The Human Factor in Management Systems. Journal of Systems Management, Vol. 22, No 11, pp. 10–15.

National Aeronautics and Space Administration, 1970. What NASA/RECON Can Do For You. NASA, Washington, D.C.

Neel, C.W., 1971. Counter Conduct in Mechanical Systems. Journal of Systems Management, Vol. 22, No 12, pp. 35–38.

Nielsen, N.R., 1974. Network Computing. In: M. Greenberger et al. (eds.), Networks for Research and Education, Sharing of Computers and Information Resources Nationwide, MIT, Cambridge, Mass.

Nielsen, N.R., 1974. The Implication of Star Computing Networks. In: IFIP Proc., Stockholm.

Optner, S.L., 1965. Systems Analysis for Business and Industrial Problem Solving. Prentice-Hall, Englewood Cliffs, N.J., 116 pp.

Polya, G., 1957. How to Solve It. Doubleday Anchor Books, Garden City, N.Y., 253 pp.

Rees, A.M., 1972. Interface of Technical Libraries with Other Information Systems. Information Pt 2, Reports Bibliographies, Vol. 1, No 1, Science Associates/International Inc., pp. 1–75.

Riley, W.B., 1971. Minicomputer Networks—a Challenge to Maxicomputers. Electronics.

Rubin, M.D., 1973. Systems in Society. SGSR, Society for General Systems Research, Washington, D.C., 312 pp.

Samuelson, K., 1968. Information Structure and Decision Sequence. In: K. Samuelson (ed.), Mechanized Information Storage, Retrieval and Dissemination, North-Holland, Amsterdam, pp. 622–636.

Samuelson, K., 1969a. Systems Design Concepts for Automated International Information Networks. In: Proceedings of ASIS Meeting, San Francisco, Volume 6, pp. 431–435.

Samuelson, K., 1969b. Automated International Information Networks, Systems Design Concepts, Goal-Setting and Priorities. FID/TM Panel at the ASIS Meeting in San Francisco, October 1969, Stockholm (TRITA-IBADB 5001), 58 pp.

Samuelson, K., 1970. World-wide Information Networks. In: Conference on Interlibrary Communications and Information Networks (CICIN), Airlie House, Warrenton, Va, September/October 1970, Proc. American Library Association, Chicago, pp. 317–346.

Samuelson, K., 1971a. Relay-Switches and Referral Directories for International Data-Bases and Information Networks. Proc. FID/CCC:CR:TM International Symposium in Herceg Novi, Yugoslavia, June/July 1971, 11 pp.

Samuelson, K., 1971b. International Information Transfer and Network Communication. In: C. Cuadra (ed.), Annual

Review of Information Science and Technology, Chapter 6, Vol. 6, Britannica, Chicago, pp. 277–324.

Samuelson, K., 1971c. Information Science University Program, Developed through a Digested Projection from European and U.S. Trends. Proceedings of a Symposium for Educators by ASIS-ALA, Denver, Co., November 1971 (ERIC, EDO61947), pp. 143–151.

Samuelson, K., 1973. Global Networks for Information, Communications and Computers. In: A. Debons and W. Cameron (eds.), Perspectives in Information Science, Noordhoff, Groningen, pp. 349–364.

Samuelson, K., 1974. Communicating within a World System. In: ICCC Proceedings 2nd International Conference on Computer Communication, Stockholm, pp. 359–366.

Samuelson, K., 1975a. International Networks for Global and Regional Resource Sharing. In: Proceedings, the Interactive Library, Computerized Processes in Library and Information Networks, UNESCO Seminar, November 25–28, 1974 in Stockholm, TLS, the Swedish Society for Technical Documentation, Stockholm, pp. 49–66.

Samuelson, K., 1975b. Information Ordering in World-wide Communications. Proceedings, Conference on Ordering Systems for Global Information Networks, Organized by FID/CR:LD:TM jointly in Bombay, January 1975, pp. 274–324.

Samuelson, K., 1975c. An Informatics Curriculum and its Similarity to Other International University Programs. Proceedings, IFIP 2nd World Conference on Computers in Education, Marseille, France, September 1975, North-Holland, Amsterdam, pp. 255–262.

Samuelson, K., Borko, H., Tell, B.V., Nador, P., Dubon, R., Irick, P.E., Mongar, H.F. and Dammers, H.F., 1971. Global and Long-distance Decision-making, Environmental Issues & Network Potentials. FID/TM Panel at the ASIS Meeting in Denver, November 1971, Stockholm (FID Publ. No 493, TRITA-IBADB 5003), 83 pp.

Samuelson, K., Heilprin, L., Nador, P., Gopnik, M., Schultz, C.K. and Heaps, D., 1972. Systems, Cybernetics and Information Networks. FID/TM, Stockholm (FID Publ. No 498, TRITA-IBADB 5004), 97 pp.

Samuelson, K., Gezelius, R., Werner, H. and Johannesson, N.O., 1972. Mixed Multimedia, Development Potentials for Picture-phone, CATV and Teleprocessing. FID/TM, Stockholm (FID Publ. No 499, TRITA-IBADB 5005), 68 pp.

Samuelson, K., et al., 1974. Evaluation of IR Systems, a User-oriented Approach for Scandinavia. NORDFORSK, Stockholm (TRITA-IBADB 5007), 146 pp.

Saracevic, T., 1971. Five Years, Five Volumes and 2345 Pages of the Annual Review of Information Science and Technology, Information Storage and Retrieval, Vol. 7, pp. 127–139.

SATCOM, 1969. Report—Committee on Scientific and Technical Communication. National Academy of Sciences, Washington, D.C.

Schoderbek, P., Kefalas, A. and Schoderbek, C., 1975. Management Systems, Conceptual Considerations. Business Publ., Dallas, Texas, 370 pp.

Simon, H. A., 1970. The Science of the Artificial. M.I.T. Press, Cambridge, Mass., 123 pp.

Toman, J., 1970. The Influence of Information Retrieval on the Structure of Indexing and Classification Systems. Proceedings, 2nd Anglo-Czech. Conference of Information Specialists, Lockwood, London, pp. 57–66.

UNESCO (United Nations Educational, Scientific and Cultural Organization), 1970. Meeting of Governmental Experts on International Arrangements in the Space Communication Field. UNESCO House, Paris, December 1969, UNESCO, Paris (Final report) (COM/MD/15), 11 pp.

Van Gigch, J. P., 1974. Applied General Systems Theory. Harper and Row, New York, 439 pp.

Vickery, B.C., 1973. Information Systems. Butterworth, London, 350 pp.

Waggener, R.C., 1974. Restoring Systems Tarnished

Charisma. Journal of Systems Management, Vol. 25, No 10, pp. 22–26.

Wagner, H.M., 1971. The ABC's of Operations Research. Operations Research (ORSA), Vol. 19, pp. 1259–82.

Weinberg, G.M., 1975. An Introduction to General Systems Thinking. Wiley, New York, 279 pp.

# Glossary

The below glossary and definitions of concepts or terms used throughout the book stem from the authors' earlier writings as well as from the P.D. (i.e. Public Domain terminology) and a number of sources that have appeared valuable in past experiences of General Systems and Information Networks. In particular, acknowledgment is given to the following basic works[1]:

*Information Systems—Data Processing and Evaluation,* by G. Dippel and W.C. House.
*Fundamentals of Systems Analysis,* by J.M. Fitzgerald and A.F. Fitzgerald.
*Management Systems, Conceptual Considerations,* by P.P. Schoderbek, A.G. Kefalas and C.G. Schoderbek.
*The Information Center—Management's Hidden Asset,* by M.F. Meltzer.
*Communication Networks for Computers,* by D.W. Davies and D. Barber.
*Future Developments in Telecommunications,* by J. Martin.
*Information Systems—Theory and Practice,* by J.G. Burch and F.R. Strater.

---

[1]See section of bibliographic references.

Alternate Routing. An alternative communications path used if the normal one is not available. There may be one or more possible alternative paths.

Bandwidth. The range of frequencies available for signaling. The difference expressed in cycles per second (hertz) between the highest and lowest frequencies of a band.

Batch Processing. The accumulating of transactions or records for a given period, then sorting into the same sequence as the master file and processing in one computer run.

Baud. The unit of signalling speed. The speed in bauds is the number of signal elements per second. Since a signal element can represent more than one bit the term baud is not always synonymous with bits per second.

Black Box Technique. The study of the relations between the experimenter and the object as well as the study of what information comes from the object, and how it is obtained.

Broadband. Communication channel having a bandwidth greater than a voice-grade channel, and therefore capable of higher-speed data transmission.

Buffer. A store, usually associated with a peripheral device or communication link, which accomodates changes or differences of data rate.

Carrier. A communication channel suitable for the transmission of electrical signals generated by the modulation of an audio wave or other stimuli.

Central Processing Unit (CPU). (1) The part of a computer that contains the circuits that control the entire operation of the computer system. (2) The arithmetic/logical unit and the control section of a computer.

Channel. (1) A communication path for transmission of data between two or more points. Also called a facility, line, link, or path. (2) A row or path along which data, usually in the form of bits, are recorded into a medium. (3) The horizontal row running across the length of paper tape.

Channel capacity. A term in data transmission used to

express the maximum number of bits per second which can be accomodated by a channel. This maximum number is determined by the bandwidth modulation scheme and certain types of noise. The channel capacity may be measured in bits per second usually as Bauds.

Channel, Multiplexor. A channel which permits several input-output devices to make use of one channel simultaneously.

Channel, Voice-grade. A channel suitable for transmission of speech, digital or analog data, or facsimile, generally with a frequency range of about 300 to 2400 cycles per second.

Circuit. A means of both-way communication between two points, comprising associated "go" and "return" channels.

Compatibility. Degree in which hardware and software of one model computer can be interchanged with hardware and software of another model computer.

Configuration. A group of machines which are interconnected and are programmed to operate as a system.

Congestion. Any communication network has a limit to the traffic it can carry. Beyond that limit the network must somehow restrict traffic. Congestion means the condition in which traffic is thus restricted.

Cybernetic System. A system characterized by extreme complexity, probabilism, and self-regulation.

Cybernetics. (1) The theory of communication and control in animal (man) and machine. (2) The comparative study of the control and the internal communication of information-handling machines and the central nervous systems of animals and man in order to understand better the function of human and mechanical systems.

Data-Base. (1) A concept whereby all data for an entire information system are located in a common file rather than separate files. (2) Also called Data-Bank. A set of logically connected files that have a common access. They are the sum total of all the data that exist within an organization.

Data-Base Administration. Arbitrator of conflicting user needs; his or her functions also include organizing, monitoring, and re-organizing the data-base system.

Decentralized. Each department or unit of the organization performs its own data processing function.

Design. A creative process which plans or arranges the parts into a whole that satisfies the objectives involved.

Diagnostic Programs. These are used to check equipment malfunctions and to pinpoint faulty components. They may be used by the computer engineer or may be called in by the supervisory programs automatically.

Diagnostics, System. Rather than checking one individual component, system diagnostics utilize the whole system in a manner similar to its operational running. Programs resembling the operational programs will be used rather than systematic programs that run logical patterns. These will normally detect overall system malfunctions but will not isolate faulty components.

Dial-up. The use of a dial or pushbutton telephone to initiate a station-to-station telephone call.

Disk Pack. A portable set of magnetic disks which may be removed from the disk drive unit, allowing another set of disks to be placed on the unit.

Display Media. The medium upon which an information output is presented either for human or machine use.

Distributed System. Each department maintains its own data base and processing procedures for its own needs but still provides for particular information to flow throughout the entire organization.

Down Time. The time during which a computer is malfunctioning or not operating correctly due to mechanical or electronic failure as opposed to available, idle, or stand-by time during which the computer is functional.

Emergency. Whatever is necessary to repair an existing malfunctioning element of the system.

Empire Builder. The type of person who seeks personal

power, prestige, and recognition through authority and control to enlarge his domain.

Environment of a System.   That which not only lies outside the system's control but which also determines in some way how the system performs.

Evaluation Criteria.   Performance standards through which management can have a valid measurement to evaluate the new system's performance.

Facsimile (Fax).   Transmission of images, pictures, maps, diagrams, etc. by communications channels. The image is scanned at the transmitter, reconstructed at the receiving station, and duplicated on some form of paper.

Fail softly.   When a piece of equipment fails, the programs let the system fall back to a degraded mode of operation rather than let it fail catastrophically and give no response to its users.

Feasibility Study.   A study projecting how a proposed system might operate in a particular organization. The study is made to provide a basis for deciding on whether and how the existing system should be changed.

Feedback.   (1) Partial reversion of the effects of a given process to its source. (2) The part of a communication system which returns the receiver's response toward the message to the source. (3) Control of a system by the output of the system—that is, a self-correcting or self-compensating control. (4) Results of past decisions or actions are used to help make future decisions.

File.   (1) An organized collection of data directed toward some purpose. (2) A logically related group of data records.

File Integrity.   A term generally used in records retention to mean that all records are in their proper location; thus, file integrity is lost when records are misfiled.

Flow Control.   In data communication networks which employ storage there is a possibility of congestion if more data flows into a node than flows out of it. To remove this possibility, flow control is needed.

Follow-up. After implementation, the analyst returns to observe actual operation of the installed system to find out if the system is really working as planned.

General Systems Design Proposal. Specifies at a general level, how the proposed system will be effective.

General Systems Theory. The theory of open-organic systems which possess certain characteristics such as organization, dynamic equilibrium, self-regulation, and teleology. Its main domain is growth and evolution of general systems.

Hardware. A symbol-receiving, -processing, and -communication device. Mechanical devices that augment man's sensory and intelligence capacities.

Heuristic Routing. A routing method in which delay data produced by normal data-carrying packets coming in on different links from a given source node are used to guide the outgoing packets as to the best link for getting to that node.

Host Computer. A computer which (in addition to providing a local service) acts as "host" to a communication computer (IMP) that gives it access to many other "hosts" via the network.

IMP. Interface Message Processor or IMP is the name of a data switching centre of the ARPA network. The network is sponsored by the Advanced Research Project Agency of the U.S.

Implementation. Consists of the installation of the new system and the removal of the current system.

Informatics. Informatics stands for Information Science and Technology, defined as that field which includes: Structure and properties of information and communication as well as theory and methods for the transfer, organizing, storage, retrieval, evaluation and distribution of information, and furthermore information systems, nets, processes and activities that mediate knowledge from source to user and are based on general systems, cybernetics, automation, and technology for human work environments in timely and current praxis.

Information.  (1) The meaning assigned to data by known conventions. (2) Processed and evaluated data, especially as derived from a collection of documents or other graphic records. (3) Knowledge or instruction acquired by the receiver through processed data.

Information Retrieval.  The process of recovering specific information from stored data.

Information System.  (1) By information system we mean: A system of information sets needed for decision and signalling in a larger system (of which it is a subsystem) containing subsystems for collecting, storing, processing, distributing, information sets. Notice that decision processes are examples of information processes, whether performed by man or by machine. Also most information processes contain decision processes. (2) An information system is a special case of an operational system, for it comprises men, machines, materials and energy acting to transform data inputs into information outputs. Consequently information systems have many features, and problems, in common with operational systems. (3) The most generic definition of information comes from philosophy: information is knowledge for the purpose of taking effective action. It is our contention that the current philosophy underlying the design of MIS has presupposed a greatly restricted view of "knowledge", "effectiveness", "action", and "purpose". More specifically, we propose that an information system consists of at least one person of a certain psychological type who faces a problem within some organizational context for which he needs evidence to arrive at a solution (i.e. to select some course of action) and that the evidence is made available to him through some mode of presentation.

In-Plant System.  A system whose parts, including remote terminals, are all situated in one building or localized area. The term is also used for communication systems spanning several buildings and sometimes covering a large distance, but in which no common carrier facilities are used.

Input.   (1) The data fed into the computer system, in the form of numbers or letters from media such as punched paper tapes, magnetic tapes, punched cards. (2) The device or set of devices used to bring data into another device. (3) Data transferred from auxiliary or external storage into internal storage.

Input-Output (I/O).   (1) A general term for the equipment used to communicate with a computer. (2) The data involved in such communication. (3) The medium carrying such data. (4) The activity of reading or writting such data.

Intelligent Terminal.   A terminal that is programmable and can process its messages, for example to check validity.

Interface.   (1) A boundary between two pieces of equipment across which all the signals which pass are carefully defined. The definition includes the connector signal levels, impedance, timing, sequence of operation and the meaning of signals. The term has been extended to include the idea of a software interface. The essence of an interface is its accurate definition. (2) A common boundary between two or more items of equipment. An interface may be mechanical—such as the physical surfaces and spacings in mating parts, modules, components, or subsystems—or electrical—such as the matching of signal levels or power levels of two or more subsystems.

Interface Computer.   Part of a packet switching network which mediates between network subscriber and the high-level or trunk network. It can be regarded as containing a local area switch and terminal processors.

Interrogative Method of Providing Information.   The idea behind this method is for the user to submit his inquiry to an access device or interface and the information will be returned in a relevant time period.

Item, Data.   (1) A single character or a group of characters which, when used in a certain context, convey meaning to the receiver. (2) A data unit which is complete within itself. Items are stored within one record on tape and may be further subdivided into fields.

Key. (1) That part of a word, record, file, etc. by which it is identified or controlled. (2) To code information. (3) A lever on a manually operated machine, as a key on a typewriter or a key punch.

Library. (1) A collection of documents for study or reference. (2) An organized collection of standard, checked-out routines. (3) A set or collection of standardized programs by which frequently occurring types of problems may be solved. The library may be catalogued according to the type of arithmetical operation employed.

Link. In one sense it is the physical communication path between two "nodes" or switching centres. In a different sense it means a conceptual link between two parties in a packet switching network, signifying that they are in communication with each other. The "parties" may be subscribers, or processes within the subscribers computers.

Line, Dedicated Private. A communications line that is assigned to the exclusive use of a particular company for its own activities. Such a line may be leased from a common carrier or constructed by the company itself.

Maintainability. Mean time to repair a malfunctioning element is usually referred to as a measure of the system's maintainability.

Management by Exception. Reporting only those items (good or bad) which deviate from the normal mode of operation.

Management Information System. (1) An information network designed to provide the right information to the right person at the right time. (2) A system in which management or others having an established need to know are provided with historical information, information on current status, and projected information appropriately summarized. A decisionmaking tool.

Mean Time Before Failure (MTBF). The average length of time for which the system, or a component of the system, works without fault.

Mean Time To Repair (MTTR). When the system, or a

component of the system, develops a fault, this is the average time taken to correct the fault.

**Message.** (1) A series of words, symbols, electrical impulses or holes intended to convey information. (2) As used in message switching, a message consists of a Header, the Text, and an End-Of-Text Indicator.

**Message Switching.** The technique of receiving a message, storing it until the proper outgoing line is available, and then retransmitting. No direct connection betweeen the incoming and outgoing lines is set up as in line switching (q.v.).

**Microcard.** A term generally used for the type of microform which is opaque as opposed to transparent. These vary a great deal in size and reduction ratio.

**Microfiche.** (1) A unitized type of microform with a number of images arranged in rows on a transparent card. (2) A $4'' \times 6''$ sheet of microfilm usually containing copies of 58 standard $8\frac{1}{2}'' \times 11''$ pages; any sheet of microfilm.

**Microfilm.** A continuous strip of film, usually either 16-mm or 35-mm, with all the "pages" placed in order. The film is usually placed on some type of reel for easy wind and rewind.

**Microform.** Any facsimile of material that is reduced in physical size so as to require special equipment to view it, as in the case of microfiche, microfilm, and aperture cards.

**Modularity.** Allows for the addition of faster or more extensive equipment to an existing configuration without the need to replace the entire system.

**Multiplexing.** (1) The process of transferring data from several storage devices operating at relatively low transfer rates in such a manner that the high-speed device is not obliged to wait for the low-speed units. (2) The division of a transmission facility into two or more channels. In telephone and telegraph, the simultaneous transmission of several messages on the same circuit. In radio and television, the simultaneous transmission of two or more independent signals on the same carrier waves.

Multiplexor. A device which uses several communication channels at the same time, and transmits and receives messages and controls the communication lines. This device itself may or may not be a stored-program computer.

Modem. (1) Contraction of modulator-demodulator. (2) A device which bi-directionally modulates and demodulates signals transmitted over communication facilities permitting two-way communications between sender and receiver.

Network. (1) Network is a distribution system composed of interlinked, spatially dispersed channels, subsystems and/or elements; but not all systems show a network structure i.e. the systems do not always have meshs or coils. The network can also be regarded as a distributing subsystem as part of some larger system. (2) Network and its channels are composed of a single route in physical space, or multiple interconnected routes, by which markers bearing information are transmitted to all parts of the organization. (3) Two or more libraries and/or other organizations engaged in a common pattern of information exchange, through communications, for some functional purpose. A network usually consists of a formal arrangement whereby materials, information, and services provided by a variety of libraries and/or other organizations are made available to all potential users. (Libraries may be in different jurisdictions but agree to serve one another on the same basis as each serves its own constituents. Computers and telecommunications may be among the tools used for facilitating communication among them.)

Node. In a topological description of a network a node is a point of junction of the links. The word has also come to mean a switching centre in the context of data networks, particularly in the context of packet switching.

Objectives. As used in systems, what one intends to accomplish in the problem definition phase or during a full systems study.

On-Line. The operation of input-output devices under the direct control of the central processor.

On-Line, Real-Time Processing. An information system that permits the processing of data to coincide with the generation of data in such a manner that information outputs are available in time to affect a process that is in progress.

Optical Character Recognition (OCR). (1) The technique of using electronic devices and light in order to detect, recognize, and translate into machine language, characters which have been printed or written on paper documents in a human-readable form. (2) The conversion of human-readable language into a machine language.

Packet. A block of data handled by a network in a well-defined format including a heading. A maximum size of packet is set, and messages longer than that size have to be carried as several packets.

Packet Switching Network. A network designed to carry data in the form of packets. The packet and its format is internal to that network. The external interfaces may handle data in different formats, for example byte by byte.

Phase-In Conversion. Procedure in which parts of the new system techniques are interfaced in order to operate with the old system; thereafter those parts of the old system still remaining are replaced with the new system completing the conversion process.

Phase-Out. By some preplanned date the old system should no longer be operating. Phasing out can pertain to parallel conversion where the old and new system are operated simultaneously until the new system has been proven. The old is generally then phased out.

Processing. That activity in the input/output cycle which transforms the input into an output.

Project Manager. A systems approach whereby one individual, the project manager, has full authority and responsibility over all people and activities within the project. This horizontal project organization implies extension of the project manager's authority over all, within and outside the organization, involved in the project.

Protocol.   A strict procedure required to initiate and maintain communication. Protocols may exist at many levels in one network such as link-by-link, end-to-end and subscriber-to-switch.

Real Time.   A real-time computer system may be defined as one that controls an environment by receiving data, processing them, and returning the results sufficiently quickly to affect the functioning of the environment at that time.

Receiver.   The target or destination in a communication system for which a message is intended.

Record.   (1) Verb: The act of registering or entering data on some appropriate medium or document. (2) Noun: A group of related facts, data items, or fields of information treated as a unit.

Redundancy.   (1) That portion of the total data contained in a message which can be eliminated without the loss of essential information. (2) The occurrence of a statement or elements of data more than once.

Re-evaluation.   After implementation and follow-up, the analyst makes whatever changes are needed for the refinement and improvement of the new system. Some portions may be redesigned and others may be revised.

Routing, Alternate.   Assignment of a secondary communications path to a destination when the primary path is unavailable.

Routing Table.   A table associated with a node which states for each packet destination the preferred outgoing link that the packet should use. Synonymous with 'directory'.

Retrieval and Display.   The output of information and its forms of presentation to the receiver in an information system.

Response Time.   The time interval between the initiation of a request of the information system and receipt of an answer.

Satisfice.   To choose a particular level of performance for which to strive and for which management is willing to settle.

Scientific Method. Method utilizing the following steps: Observation, Formulation of a Model, Testing the Model, and Application or Implementation.

Selective Dissemination of Information (SDI). A methodology whereby key words are submitted to an information retrieval system and documents containing these key words are located and returned to the user.

Software. A set of computer programs, procedures, and possibly associated documentation concerned with the operation of a data processing system, e.g., compilers, library routines, manuals, circuit diagrams. Contrasted with hardware.

System. A set of objects, together with relationships between the objects and between their attributes, connected or related to each other and to their environment in such a manner as to form an entirety or whole.

Systems Analysis. (1) The steps or operations involved in studying the characteristics of a problem. (2) The examination of an activity, procedure, method, technique, or business to analyze existing operations and determine how they can be better accomplished. (3) The organized step-by-step study of the detailed procedures for the collection, manipulation, and evaluation of data about an organization for the purpose of determining not only what must be done but also to ascertain the best way to improve the functioning of the system.

Systems Analyst. A methods person who can start with a complex problem, break it down, and identify the solutions.

Systems Approach. (1) A methodology of problem solving which involves an analysis of the present system and subsequently, an improved design of a new system. (2) A philosophy that conceives of an organization as a set of objects with a given set of relationships between the objects and their attributes, connected or related to each other and to their environment in such a way as to form a whole or entirety.

System Design. (1) The design of some man–machine combination to carry out a needed set of operational tasks. (2) A plan, procedure, and/or description of a new system which will supplant or improve upon an existing system. (3) The art of developing a new system. Ten steps outlined portray the systems design cycle. It is concerned with the coordination of activities, job procedures, and equipment utilization in order to achieve organizational objectives.

System, Proposed. The newly developed system designed to replace the existing (current) system.

Table Lookup. (1) A computer search to obtain a function value corresponding to an argument, stated or implied, from a table of function values stored in the computer. (2) The operation of obtaining a value from a table.

Teleprocessing. A form of information handling in which a data processing system utilizes communication facilities.

Terminal. Any device capable of sending and/or receiving information over a communication channel. The means by which data are entered into a computer system and by which the decisions of the system are communicated to the environment it affects. A wide variety of terminal devices have been built, including teleprinters, special keyboards, light displays, cathode ray tubes, thermocouplers, pressure gauges and other instrumentation, radar units, telephones, walkie-talkie-lookies etc.

Terminal Processor. In a packet switching network it is convenient to treat terminals like other processors needing communication. To this end, each terminal has a process looking after it. This can be regarded as residing in a terminal processor (a separate processor is not essential—it could be part of an interface computer, for example).

TIP. Terminal interface processor i.e. a terminal IMP.

Transceiver. A terminal that can transmit and receive traffic.

Ultrafiche. One of the newer types of photoreduction onto

microform. Similar to microfiche in that it is transparent; but because of the method of reduction, many more frames can be "packed" onto a single 4×6 inch or 3×6 inch transparency.

Update. To modify a master file with current data from a transaction file according to a specified procedure.

# Index

145